FOR NANCY

AUTHOR'S NOTE

The three plays included here, "Dream of a Blacklisted Actor," "Defense of Taipei", and "Mayday" were either written in the 1950's or are set in that decade. They do not stand with each other as sequels but on their own. The young man Joe in "Mayday" is related to his namesake in "Dream of a Blacklisted Actor." In the last mentioned play the notion of "Dream" means people performing in realistic behavior in unrealistic circumstances. Where they sing, it should be simply accepted by the other characters as them speaking. As in our dreams we perform naturally in unnatural settings that do change magically, much like an editor's jump cut in films.

"Mayday" is a comedy, "Taipei," a dark comedy, and "Dream" is not so funny at all. Except in spots.

Conrad Bromberg- 1-10-13

DREAM OF A BLACKLISTED ACTOR

BY

CONRAD BROMBERG

© 2011 Conrad Bromberg
Conrad Bromberg
PO box 570
GreatBarrington,
MA 01230

Phone: 413-528-4785
Fax: 413-528-4785

ISBN: 061563415X
ISBN 13: 9780615634159

PROLOGUE

EDWARD MORRIS, a leonine man in
his mid-fortiesdressed in bright colors, enters in a follow-spot and sings
the following.

ED

When I was seven and an orphan in an immigrant world,
I was sent to a family in Astoria, New York,
I worked, cleaning the house.
Once, one of their children filched a quarter
From the hanging pants of the father,
He blamed me and locked me in a closet
Till I confessed the crime.
By eight of the evening hunger showed me my father,
By eleven thirst brought my dead mother,
By midnight I was in the world of light,
By noon the next day,
When the woman brought me out,
I knew the nature of light.

When I was fifteen and a night worker in a laundry,
I lived with my sister and daytime went to high school,
One night I grew sweaty and cold with fever,
I asked to go home,
But the owner resented the fact that I spoke fluent English.
He turned me down.
At eight o'clock I was one hundred point two and sluggish,
I visited with King Lear,
By one AM while on the subway making love to Lady Macbeth,
I slipped off the seat and was left on the floor.
Horatio and I staggered through the snow to my sister's.
Though I came through the fever with a heart like a leaky
Parachute,I knew the nature of light.
When I was twenty-seven and an actor downtown,
Outside our cellar the country was depressed,

ED(CONT'D)

But in our cellar were scraggly faced actors
Who didn't care for each other and
Were constantly stealing each other's women,
Who also cared little for each other or us.
But in that room beneath the street,
Each night we stood upon our feet and spoke of our time.
At eight o'clock the room was dim,
By nine we moved in candlelight,
By ten we had invented electricity,
And by eleven, with the brightness, the brightness,
We knew the nature of light.

When I was forty-one and lived on a hilltop in Hollywood,
The shock of sudden stardom had leveled off
To days in the sun reading Balzac and sipping tequila,
And nights was the group, full of Marxist discussion,
A sport-coated writer who lectured on hunger,
An actor in polo pants who talked on injustice,
And I played believer. I still play the part.
And by nine the room lights failed to rise,
And by eleven I left my hilltop home
And went on a drive to see if a woman could bring back
My knowledge of the nature of light.

Now I am forty-six and an exile from hilltops,
I dwell in five rooms in my youth-spent Manhattan,
Gone are the savings from years in the sunlight,
And parachute valves in my heart leave congestion,
And illiterate congressmen resent my good English,
When I tell them I oppose their war in Korea,
And my name is on lists that are locked in desk drawers,
And there's silence in offices when my name is mentioned,
But I haven't forgotten that when I worked,
At eight o'clock the room was dim,

ED(CONT'D)

By nine I spoke with my mother,
At ten I visited King Lear,
And by eleven, with the brightness, the brightness,
I knew the nature of light.Here's an arrogant premise. "If you know the nature of light, bow your head to no man." Let's see how it works out. The first part is titled "The Struggle of Love Against Chaos."

(He does a theatrical flourish)
Para-pati, para-patu!

LIGHTS:Up on MORRIS APARTMENT.

ACT I

(The family is seated in a freeze position at the dinner table.)

ED

(as HE goes to table to sit)
This is my family.

(Gestures to COOKIE, an attractive woman in her early forties; to TERESA, a near obese girl in her early twenties, but with a pretty face; to JOE, a lanky, over-friendly boy of twenty, and in JOE's lap, a wild, red-haired puppet, FRANZ. They unfreeze as HE sits, and begin eating)
I went down to Stone's office this morning. I thought, what the hell, maybe the phone approach is too oblique. Maybe I should confront him directly. But not too directly. So I waited in a doorway across the street from his building for his car to arrive.

FRANZ

The king hiding in a doorway!

ED

Not hiding, casually waiting.

FRANZ

Proudly waiting!

                    TERRY
            (to JOE)
Will you let him tell the story?

                    JOE
            (to FRANZ)
Will you be quiet?

                    FRANZ
Gimme a kiss, big fella.

                    COOKIE
Joe...

                    JOE
            (pointing at FRANZ)
It's him, not me.

                    ED
May I continue?

                    JOE
Sorry, Dad. Sure.

                    ED
So I waited for him. The idea was that when he got out of the car
to cross those twelve steps to the building, I would accidentally
appear, as if I was simply out for a walk. We'd get to chatting,
go up to his office, he'd make an offer and I'd come home with a
contract in my pocket.

                    COOKIE
What happened?

                    ED
It didn't quite work out that way. I waited almost an hour,
pretending to look in store windows, various such activities,
always an eye out for his car. When he finally did pull up, I started
to cross, when suddenly there was an absolute avalanche of
traffic! On this quiet little side street, out of nowhere every car in
the city was blaring by! I couldn't cross the street!

                    JOE
And he went in the building and never saw you?

ED

Couldn't cross the street!

FRANZ

One more part of the conspiracy!

ED

(Laughs)

Even the vehicles are against me!

TERRY

(with an evil leer)

There they were, all those sneaky trucks and buses, waiting, crouched in alleys...

ED

Waiting for me to touch toe to cobblestone...

TERRY

Then, whoom! Down they come!

ED

Vroom! Vroom!

COOKIE

(half-laughing)

Well, Ed, we know that trucks have had it in for you for years!

(THEY ALL laugh)

ED

And the buses! I've always said that buses as a class were politically unreliable!

JOE

And those sneaking sonsabitching little cars, too!

TERRY

Vreem! Vreem!

ED

That's right! Vreem, vreem, the little rats! Cars are nothing but a bunch of goddam opportunists! The trucks at least had a political position, vroom, vroom, El Capitalismo! But those vreem, vreeming little bastards were just in there sucking up to the big boys!

ED(CONT'D)
(THEY ALL laugh. It subsides)
So, what did everybody do today?
COOKIE
Worked.

JOE
Slept.
ED
(drily)
I see, sheer excitement. Terry?
(on mention of her name, COOKIE and JOE freeze.
TERRY rises and puts on her coat and picks up a
Package and moves out of the dining area to the street.)
ED
(to audience)
She's remembering. I don't know about this yet, but I will.

LIGHTS:Up on dusky STREET.

(TERRY walks along the street on her way home
in an autumn sunset.An ascetic looking MAN in a dark suit
approaches her. HE is notable for his luminous green eyes)

KIEHL
Excuse me, young lady.
TERRY
(a bit startled)
Yes?
KIEHL
I think I saw you on television a few years ago. Is your father
Edward Morris?
TERRY
Yes, he is.
KIEHL
(very friendly)

KIEHL(CONT'D)

Of course. How is he?

TERRY

Fine. Do you know him?

KIEHL

Yes, very well. We were "active" together back in Hollywood. What's he doing now?

TERRY

Well, acting.

KIEHL

Is he still a communist?

TERRY

No, he left some...
            (realizes her admission, horrified)
Who are you?

KIEHL
            (his tone suddenly insistent)
Was Robert Coles in your father's cell in the Party?!

TERRY
            (backing away)
Who are you?

KIEHL
            (pursuing her)
James Nettles?

TERRY
            (running off)
Oh, God...

KIEH
            (not chasing, calling after her, laughing)
Angela Dean? George Steinberg?!
            (The street section goes dark. TERRY returns
to the dining table and removes her coat. JOE and COOKIE
unfreeze.)

ED

Terry? What did you do today?

TERRY

(seated, not looking up from her plate)

Nothing.

FRANZ

A quiet day in the kingdon.

ED

(to audience)

How would you like some music?

(Instantly the FAMILY leaves the dining area and crosses to the living area where some chairs are set up for a chambermusic group.COOKIE sits, as audience, across from chairs. JOE sets FRANZ down next to her. ED, TERRY, and JOE sit in the chairs.)

What'll it be?

COOKIE

A little Bach, please.

ED

(to the other TWO)

Bach?

(THEY nod)

Ready? And...

(THEY proceed to improvise a fugue in the style of Johann Sebastian Bach. JOE plays violin. TERRY plays harpsichord. ED plays cello. Their voices emit the lyrically contrapuntal notes, as THEY finger their imaginary instruments. The piece continues as the area fadesTo darkness. Out of it, ED steps forward.To audience)

We began our little chamber group some years ago when the children were still in school. We would sit out at the pool of an evening and let the melodies carry down the canyon and out toward the waters of the Pacific. It was leisurely and pleasant, a gentle coda to mark the end of the day.

ED(CONT'D)
(HE steps back into the dark area.When the lights rise again, we see them by the pool. Behind them a pink and purple Western sunset. THEY conclude the piece, and COOKIE applauds gently. There is a moment of silence as THEY behold the sunset.)

We see their appearances are
Altered. COOKIE is younger
Looking, in a soft, blue sweater.
JOE, too, in his letterman's sweater.
TERRY, in a pretty dress of the 1940's, Is not
heavy, but with her smock off,Slightly plump.
ED wears a white terry-Cloth full length robe.

COOKIE
(Reclining, releasing her thoughts to the sunset)
When I was a child in Brooklyn, I never dreamed of this kind of beauty. Two weeks every summer we went to the mountains. With our luck it rained most of the time.
Through high school my most cherished memory of nature was a rainbow I'd seen when I was nine. The rest was the grocery store and the crowded streets. We weren't sad, though. We knew we were rising. We always had hope. But this, I never dreamed of it.

ED
It is a dream.
COOKIE
I know, but I love it.
ED
(To the sky)
Dream on, my queen, and let not hell
Disrupt your discourse with heaven.

TERRY
Mom, how did you and Dad meet?
COOKIE
(Thinks, then)

COOKIE(CONT'D)

We were very young. We were both counselors at a camp. Your father raped me. That began a long and glorious relationship.

ED

It was not rape.

COOKIE

It was our day off. The campers were off on a hike. It was the middle of the afternoon, and we were sitting on his bunk. He was orating on the relation of art to reality, which was a very popular topic at the time. In the midst of a sentence, he stopped, and with not so much as a beg-pardon-madam, threw me down on the bunk and took his pleasure.

ED

Ask her if she resisted.

COOKIE

It was a sneak attack. I was too surprised.

ED

So surprised, she herself undid the buttons on her shorts.

COOKIE

He was frothing at the mouth. I was afraid of violence.

ED

She chased me around that camp for five weeks. She was a pitiable site, whimpering like a sick dog at my door. What I did, I did out of pity. No decent man could've done less.

COOKIE

(sighs pleasurably)

Have it as you wish.

ED

(Smiles)

I did. And I do.

COOKIE

(Smiles)

Leave me to my sunset.

(THEY ALL return to watch the dying rays. THEY are silhouettedagainst the sky for a moment as the lights fade to:)

BLACKOUT

LIGHTS:Follow spot back upon ED.
(HE comes out in his regular dress,To audience)

ED

And now, "Blacklist Blackouts!"
                    The following vignettes are
                    done in almost vaudeville tempo.

LIGHTS:Up on ED and COOKIE in limbo spot.
ED

Herb Lewis thinks he may be on a list.

COOKIE

He never had a political thought in his life.

ED

He was working steadily, then four months ago it went dead.

COOKIE

Why?

ED

He thinks the producers are confusing him with Herman Lewis
who's on all the lists.

COOKIE

What's he doing about it?

ED

Going from office to office trying to clear it up.

COOKIE

That's good.

ED

No, it's not.

COOKIE

Why not?

ED

When he comes to them, they deny there's a blacklist at all. When he leaves they mark him down for bad because he reminded them of what they're doing.

BLACKOUT

LIGHTS:Up on JOE and TERRY in limbo spotAcross stage.

JOE

John Ross is in the hospital.

TERRY

For what?

JOE

There was a knock on his door. When he opened the door a man punched him and beat him up.

TERRY

Who was it?

JOE

They don't know.

TERRY

Are the police looking?

JOE

Very casually.

BLACKOUT

LIGHTS:Up on ED and COOKIE in limbo spot

ED

I saw Danny Jamison today.

COOKIE

Oh, good. How is he?

ED

I don't know.

                              COOKIE
What do you mean?

                                ED
When he saw me on the street, he turned and walked in the
opposite direction.

                            BLACKOUT

                    LIGHTS: up on ED and COOKIE in limbo
                    spot.

                              COOKIE
When's the funeral?

                                ED
Day after tomorrow.

                              COOKIE
Are you going?

                                ED
Yes, we used to be close.

                    LIGHTS UP:The family dining area.

                    (The FOUR FAMILY MEMBERS move into it and
takeTheir places at the dinner table As the dialogue continues in
a More natural tone)

                                ED
And he was a lonely man.

                              COOKIE
I'd go, but...

                                ED
No, don't miss work.

                                JOE
What did the note say?

                                ED

His son was very ill in a hospital upstate. He himself hadn't worked in two years, and the usual stuff about being depressed over everything and...He was tired.

TERRY

Two years, that's nothing. You haven't worked in four!

FRANZ

But the king is tireless!

TERRY

Who do you think holds the record?

COOKIE

Terry, please...

JOE

Nora Johnson hasn't worked in five.

TERRY

Bill Standish hasn't worked in seven!

JOE

He doesn't count. He went to England. And he's working there.

TERRY

But in America, he's got seven years!

ED

Paul Tannenbaum. Ten years.

JOE

Ten years! That's before the war! What did they get him on.

ED

He was a studio carpenter. He tried to bring Negroes into the craft unions. He hasn't been let in a studio since 1941. And he's still trying.

COOKIE

My God, how does he survive?

ED

Just like we do, by hanging on.

FRANZ

Today's sermon was delivered by the Right Reverend…

COOKIE

Joseph!

JOE

It wasn't me, it was him!
(Turns puppet to him)
Watch your tongue, you scrofulous dog, or I'll saw you to death!

TERRY

(shakes her head)
Six more years, I'll be twenty-eight.
(to JOE)
You'll be twenty-six.

JOE

(To COOKIE)
You'll be forty-nine!

TERRY

(To ED)
And, Daddy, my God, you'll be fifty-two!
(SHE and JOE look aghast at their FATHER, who regards them with patient distaste)

ED

Any more good news?

FRANZ

Even kings grow old!

ED

(Jumps up, to JOE)

ED(CONT'D)

Get him out of here! If you can't keep him respectful, get him out!
I won't be baited in my own house!
(HE throws down his napkin and stalks out to the
bedroom)
Not by any goddamn sniveling boy!

(COOKIE rises, and with a withering look to JOE in
passing, crosses out following ED into the bedroom)

TERRY

(After a moment of silence)
You know, Joe, sometimes I'm not sure what side you're on.

FRANZ

Listen, fatty, why don't you go count ripples or something?

TERRY

(Rising)
You are a coward!
(SHE exits to the living room.While, in the
bedroom COOKIE stands In the doorway as ED paces)

COOKIE

Ed, please, come back. Finish your dinner.

ED

I walk the streets every day like an invisible man! I haunt their
offices! My comrades are dying! And I come home to be sniped
at! I won't tolerate it!

COOKIE

Ed, please, your heart.

ED

The hell with my heart! For the sixty measly dollars he brings in
from that goddam janitor nonsense of his, I don't have to put up
with his shit! Sixty dollars! I used to spend that much for a shirt!
A stinking piece of cloth I'd toss away like that!

COOKIE
(Crosses to him)
Ed, I beg you, calm down.

ED
If he has grievances against me, let him come out and say them!
But this eternal sniping!

COOKIE
I know...

ED
(In a calmer tone)
Most of the time I let it pass. I say, all right, that's Joe, that's his
way, ignore it. The family united, that's the only way we can win.
I believe that. A man alone is nothing. But a family united, it's
invincible. So, I ignore his jibes. But on a day like today...

COOKIE
Phil's death?

ED
He was alone, and they beat him. That's all I could think of all day.
If I didn't have you guys... I don't know what I'd do. I don't know
if I could stand up to them.

COOKIE
(Puts her arms around him)
You have us, sweetheart.

ED
But then I come home and...

COOKIE
He doesn't mean it. It's the only way he can express the father-
son thing.

ED
I carried Phil in my heart all day. He was a gentle man. You can't
be gentle in this world. They'll kill you for it.

COOKIE
(Puts her arm around him)
Come back to dinner.
(THEY walk back into the dining area arm in arm.
ED goes over to JOE)

ED
Excuse the outburst, son. I had a bad day.

JOE
(Moved, trying not to show it)
Aw, Pop, nothing to it. I understand.
(THEY embrace, but FRANZ is between them. JOE
pulls him out of the way, laughs nervously.)
Get him out of the way.
(THEY embrace fully)
I have to go to work.
ED
Go ahead, son.
The doorbell rings.

(THEY ALL turn toward it, but nobody moves.It
rings again. Still THEY don'tmove, as if disoriented by this rarely
heard sound.)

TERRY
It's the front door.
COOKIE
But the super rings the back bell.
TERRY
The meter man, too.
JOE
Who do you think it could be?
ED
(To COOKIE)
Were you expecting anyone?

COOKIE

No. Were you?

(HE shakes his head negatively. It rings again)

ED

I'll get it.

COOKIE

Be careful.

(ED opens the door, and there stands KIEHL.
TERRY gasps silently and shrinks back into her doorway)

ED
(Who seems to know him)

What do you want?

KIEHL

I was sorry to hear about Mr. Loeb. I know you and he were good friends.

ED

What's that to do with you?

KIEHL

I thought we might talk.

ED

About what?

KIEHL

My offer.

JOE
(Moves toward them)

What offer?

KIEHL

Didn't you tell them, Mr. Morris?

COOKIE

He told me.

ED
(To JOE)

It was just the usual thing, nothing big.

JOE

What was it?

ED

My name cleared.

JOE

Everywhere?

ED

Yes.

FRANZ

Ah, sunlight on the hilltops!

COOKIE

In exchange for a few names.

JOE

Public or private?

ED

In private session.

JOE

No one would know?

COOKIE

You would know, I would know.

KIEHL

Also, the small informal press conference afterward.

JOE

On television?

ED

Just the statement about my change of heart, that this time I fully cooperated with the Committee. Nothing about the names.

JOE
(Thinks, feels all eyes on him, to KIEHL)
As far as I'm concerned, mister, you can go to hell.

TERRY

I'll never betray my father! Never!

COOKIE
(Quietly, firmly)

Go away.

ED

You heard them.

KIEHL
(Nods, smiles)

Perhaps later.

(ED closes the door on KIEHL)

FRANZ

Goodbye, hilltops!

ED
(Crosses back to dining area)

Nonsense. The fact that he came here is a good sign. The hysteria is waning. Why else would he seek me out?

TERRY
(From her doorway)

Who is that man?

(As the FAMILY freezes, ED crosses out of the apartment area and onto the street, which is wintry and grey, near nightfall.)

LIGHTS: Up on ED and KIEHL in the street.

ED

Who are you?

KIEHL

My name is Kiehl.

ED

What do you want with me?

KIEHL

To help you clear yourself.

                    ED
Are you from the committee?
                    KIEHL
            (Smiles evasively)
I'm in contact with them.
                    ED
How do I know that?
                    KIEHL
There are two men who sit in a car outside your apartment
house. The ones who take the pictures of people entering and
leaving. Ask them if they know me.

                    ED
Did you put them there?
            (KIEHL again smiles enigmatically)
Why are you so interested in me?
            (KIEHL again does not answer)
Have I committed a crime?
                    KIEHL
Not that I'm aware of.
                    ED
Then why?
                    KIEHL
            (Smiles again)
You're a fascinating man. TO me, to the Committee, to the people
at large.

            LIGHTS:Fade to

            BLACKOUT

            (ED comes out of the blackout in follow spot, to
audience)

                    ED
Sometimes I like to play Balzac!

(HE crosses back into the family area, as the lights come up to reveal TERRY at her easel in herroom. It is daylight. SHE paints andlistens to ED, who marches up and down in the living room, taking on the half-dandy, half-bull qualitiesof Honore de Balzac. An imaginary WOMAN enters the room. HE turnsAnd goes to her.)

Ah, Madame de Berney, my dear madame, my dearest, caretaker of my heart and savior of my finances!

(HE kisses HER, then leads her into the room and sits her down,resumes his pacings)

You've come just in time.

(HE goes to table and picks up an imaginary letter, takes it to her)

This letter came not an hour ago. Yes, from our little friend, L'entrille. He demands ten thousand francs immediately or he and the others will move me to the bench of bankruptcy!

(SHE asks can L'entrille do it)

Can he? What can he do? He is a husk, a musk, a fig in the sun too long! Let him try it! Perhaps the effort of taking his legs to court will kill him! He does not live now! His sole act is his signature! His pleasure, forfeitures! His scrotum is a ledger! His tool a quill! He hopes to live to a hundred by the act of sitting still! And he hates me because I am out and about in the roiling world, spending my days as if they were loose coins! He is miserly with his life, and so would poison mine! Let him try, that nonce, that ponce, that squeaming little prunt!

TERRY

(Calls out)

Prunt? What's that?

ED

Take the vulgar words for the male and female organs, mix them together and you have a prunt!

(To MADAME DE BERNEY)

ED(CONT'D)

Forgive me, my dear, my daughter, sequestered in her room. Strange child, she sits for days at work on some mysterious thing and never leaves the house!

TERRY

I do so.

ED

Ah, yes, once a week the grand safari to the neighborhood art store.

TERRY

More than that.

ED

(Crosses to door to TERRY's room)

She is a recluse from the sun! Behold, madame, she lives in that filthy smock.

TERRY

I wear it when I'm working.

ED

She wears it all the time! Or the yellow one with the red smears. I never see her in a dress. I wish to see her beautiful. Like my little girl. In a pretty dress, the way she used to.

TERRY

That's nonsense, I'm too busy.

ED

(Steps into the room, as himself,directly to her)

With what?

(SHE covers the canvas SHE is working on with her body)

Why is that painting such a secret? You've been working on it for months. Why won't you show it to me?

TERRY

(Studies him now)

Are you acting now or are you real?

                    ED

I'm real. I want to know.

                  TERRY

I'm working on something. There's something I have to work out.

                    ED

What?

                  TERRY

Something private.

                    ED

Something bad.

                  TERRY

I didn't say that.

                    ED

I can see it. I see the way you are.

                  TERRY

I'm fine. Just leave me alone.

                    ED

I want to see the painting.

                  TERRY
            (Hugs it tighter)

No.

                    ED

I have the right, Terry. I'm your father.

                  TERRY

And I have the right to privacy. Isn't that what you're all about, the privacy of your thoughts? This is the privacy of my work.

                    ED

They're not the same.

                  TERRY

Why not?

                    ED

You and I are friends. The committee and I are not. I'm responsible for you.

TERRY

No, you're not. Let me do my work.

ED

Terry, I can't stand to see you this way!

TERRY

I'm fine! Go back to your acting.

ED

(Turns away)
Well, if you don't trust me...
(HE crosses back into the living room. HE
glances,looking for MADAME DE BERNEY but
can'tfind her. His thoughts on his DAUGHTER,HE
stands mutely by a table.She waits to hear his
voice resume the scene. It doesn't . After a long
moment SHE picks up the painting and carries it
into the living room)

TERRY

I do trust you.
(ED crosses to her. SHE shows him the painting.)

ED

Kiehl. Why him?

TERRY

I would never knowingly betray you. Do you believe that?

ED

Of course.

TERRY

(SHE gives him painting, paces the floor)
He tricked me. He stopped me on the street, when we first came
here and pretended he was a friend of yours. And then, suddenly,
he asked if you were still in the Party. I answered before I
thought.

ED

Bastard!

TERRY

I was so ashamed. I was afraid to tell you. I didn't mean to betray you.

ED

(Puts down painting and crosses to her, embraces her)

You didn't betray me, sweetheart. Listen to me. He didn't need that information from you. He knew I'd left the Party. They know all about me and all about my friends. When he asked you that, it was to intimidate you. It's harassment, nothing more. The same way when I leave the house and the two men follow me. It's not to see where I'm going. It's to frighten people away from me...

TERRY

He got information out of me. Now I have to deal with him.

ED

Deal with him? How?

(SHE moves out of the embrace)

TERRY

(Decides whether to tell him, then)

I have to paint the power out of his eyes.

ED

(Trying not to be shocked)

You what?

TERRY

Something in his eyes, their luminescence, their evil. I really think it was his eyes that made me answer. To say things I didn't want to.

(Looks her FATHER square in the eye)

TERRY(CONT'D)

I believe in mystical things. I believe eyes can be separate individuals placed in the bodies of other people.

ED

Alright...

TERRY

They must be dealt with mystically. That's why, if I can paint the evil power out of his eyes, I'll have conquered him. Then I can do anything I want.

ED

Like go for a walk.

TERRY

Among other things.

ED

You can do that now.

TERRY

No. Soon, though. He's clever. You see how he's resisted me for so long. But I'll get him. I will.

ED

Teresa, darling, come, put on a dress. Let me take you for a walk.

TERRY
(Shakes her head)
No. Besides, I don't have a dress.

ED

You don't? You had a closetful.

TERRY
(shrugs)
I threw them away.

ED

Threw them away? Why?!

TERRY

Daddy, please, don't shout at me. You know how it frightens me.

ED

(Hides behind Balzac)

Do you hear it, Madam, threw them away! I've squandered a fortune on silks, an this child will wear sack cloth! My progeny has prunted me. Threw them away? Why?

TERRY

(Shrugs)

I don't know.

ED

(Confused, disturbed, but plunging on)

Very well, then, just as you are, come for a walk with me.

TERRY

Dressed as you are?

ED

(Having forgotten HE was in costume)

Ah-ha! Well! If bad Balzac be barred from the salons of the rich, he will perform for the poor on the street!

(Sees her fear of such a scene,as himself)

I'll change my clothes.

TERRY

(Shakes her head)

Please, Daddy, let me do it my way.

ED

Just a little stroll.

TERRY

I can't...

ED

Down to the flower district. I know you used to love going there. Let the colors charm you, the fragrances seduce you.

TERRY

I have enough fragrances here.

ED

What do you mean?

TERRY

Yours. Tobacco and bay rum. Their odor fills the room. It keeps me company when you're not here. Can I tell you something?

ED

Yes.

TERRY

I worked all last night. In the late hours the fragrance faded. I couldn't work. Do you know what I did?

ED

What?

TERRY

I went in the bathroom and poured some on my throat here, and on my arms here, and on my hands, and on my mouth. Then I brought in a cigar and let it burn in here. It was like having you here again. I could work again.

ED

Did you sleep?

TERRY

No, I don't sleep. I just have snacks. They keep me happy.

BLACKOUT

FRANZ'S SONG

(JOE sits with FRANZ on a box. A broom leans against the box.JOE and FRANZ face the audience.)

FRANZ
(Sings in a creaky sing-song)
I know a king
Who sits on someone's head,
And when he goes to bed

FRANZ(CONT'D)

Thinks he's fine.

I know a queen
Who cries herself to sleep
Yet utters not a peep
To the man.

I know a lad
Who'd like to take a gun
And point at someone
Who sits upon his head!

I know a dummy
Who wishes he were dead,
And standing in his stead
Was the lad!

JOE

Be quiet! What the hell do you know!

FRANZ

(Turns, looks at Joe)
Look at your head, boy, flatter and flatter!

JOE

He's my father! I love him!

FRANZ

He's a tyrant!

JOE

What he's fighting for its right! I won't go against him!

FRANZ

What's he fighting for but his preening pride! The fox got caught
in the henhouse and won't admit it!

JOE

No! The right to think! The right to speak! Freely speak your mind!
(A pause as JOE hears his own words.)

FRANZ

(Sings)
I know a lad
Who'd love to speak his mind,
But at home the king ain't kind
To those who speak their mind.

JOE
(Throws FRANZ to floor)
Quiet! Not another word out of you!
(Thinks, then more quietly)
I'll go with him a little longer. I owe it to him,
(Picks up the crumbled dummy,straightens him out)
I'm sorry if I hurt you.
(Sits down with FRANZ across his lap, cradling him)
I wish I had a child instead of you. If this ever ends I'd like to get married and work in a factory and live unknown among the poor.

BLACKOUT

Scene: The Morris Apartment. After dinner.
(The Family sits around as COOKIE reads from a budget list. THEY are still at the dinner table.)

COOKIE
(Reads)
Paint materials, $29.50 last month. Why? What's the reason?
ED
Quite right. Much too much.

TERRY

It's part of my project. I simply can't stint on paint.

COOKIE

You'll have to. That's just too much.

ED

You can make do. You can mix paints for combinations.

COOKIE

Work transportation, Joseph, $37.00. How many subways does it take to get you to 28th street?

JOE

Well, I have to take the crosstown bus over to…

COOKIE

How many blocks is it?

JOE

Well, five, six…

COOKIE

Walk it.

ED

Yes, right. That's a big saving right here.

COOKIE

Cigars, $29…

ED

(Pronged)

Now wait a minute.

COOKIE

No. We're not in Hollywood anymore. No more three for a dollar. From now, if you must smoke those evil smelling things, they'll be three for a quarter.

ED

Jesus!

     (SHE is through. SHE nods to ED,Who rises and begins pacing)

Alright, here's the situation. Stone hasn't called me back in three months. I don't think it's him. I think it's his office manager. So, we move to the next position. We send a telegram. There's no name of sender on a telegram. It arrives sealed and anonymous. It can only be opened by Stone. We send it, then wait a week. If he doesn't respond, we move to the next position. Alright? "John Stone, etc., etc." What do we say?

JOE

Well, after three months of no-answer, "Dear Jack, Urgent you call me. Must make plans."

TERRY

Oh, for God's sake, it shrieks of anxiety. "Urgent, must," all wrong.

ED

Right. We must seem calm and independent. As if we are going about our business, and he's just a part of it.

TERRY

How about this? "Thought of you yesterday. Now about lunch?

ED

Mm. Not bad.

JOE

Wait a minute. Why do you need lunch? What do you want from him?

ED

Yes, good point. It's still too direct. We mustn't suggest that we have any need. Prosperity is the keynote, leisure.

     (HE paces, then stops)

I've got it! Dear Jack, weekending in Bimini. Love to all."

(The CHILDREN give their approval.COOKIE
discreetly studies her fingernails.)

BLACKOUT

LIGHTS:Up on OFFICE.

(ED comes out of darkness. HE crosses to STONE's
office. HE enters. The door to the inner Office opens. Grace, the
secretary, enters and speaks)

                    GRACE
May I help you?
                    ED
Yes. Are you Grace?
                    GRACE
Yes, I am.
                    ED
I think we've spoken on the phone. I'm Edward Morris.
            (No response)
I'm an old friend of Mr. Stone.
            (No response again)
I just dropped by to tell him I'm back from Bimini and...
            (NO response still)
Perhaps to come in and...chat.

                    GRACE
Would you have a seat, Mr. Morris?
            (The door closes and ED sits. Across stage in the
darkness
(LIGHTS:A spotlight up on TERRY in limbo)

                    TERRY
My daddy's a star. What's you daddy?
            (LIGHTS: A spotlight comes up on COOKIE in
another limbo area)

COOKIE

Our best year was, I think, 1943. We made a hundred and fifty thousand dollars after taxes.

(LIGHTS: A spotlight comes up on JOE)

JOE

Oh, hell, Dad, all the other kids have convertibles!

(In the office area a SECOND ACTOR enters and sits across from ED.)

COOKIE

...We gave a pool party for the Soviet-American Friendship Committee. The big event was the fifty-yard free style. If you won you only had to pledge five hundred dollars. Then the price went up to two thousand for the last place. Of course everyone was so drunk they couldn't swim fifty yards, so they all pledged two thousand and skipped the race. Well, why not? We made a hundred thousand that year.

ED

(To himself)

Where did it all go?

MAN

(Leans forward)

Beg pardon?

ED

(Brought out of reverie)

What? Nothing, sorry.

(A THIRD ACTOR enters and sits across from ED)

JOE

They're great, Dad, but, uh, what're you going to do with five tuxedos?

TERRY

Stupid, he's going to five parties.

COOKIE

You're both wrong. He's going to make five appearances at one party.

(The inner office door opens. The FIRST ACTOR exits.)

GRACE

Mr. Bennett, would you come in?

ED

(Rises)
Excuse me, but I was here before this gentleman.

GRACE

Did you have an appointment, sir?

ED

Well, no, I told you I just dropped by to...
GRACE

Mr. Bennett has an appointment, I'm sorry.

(MR. BENNETT now enters the inner office)

ED

(Points to THIRD ACTOR)
Does this gentleman have an appointment?

MR. WARREN

(Jumps in helpfully, to GRACE)
I'm afraid I don't. My name is Warren. Paul Warren.

ED

Then I'm next.
(No response)
TERRY

Daddy starred in nine pictures.

                              ED
Isn't that right? I'm next.
                    (No response)
                              JOE
He once threw the head of the studio out of our house. For drunk
driving, in our living room.
                    (The door to the inner office closes)

                              ED
                    (As HE resumes his seat)
Thank you.
                         MR. WARREN
Quite alright.
                    (HE returns to his magazine, then)
Excuse me, but....Aren't you Edward Morris?
                              ED
Yes, I am.
                         MR. WARREN
Of course, I remember you. You did all those "Box Car Johnny"
movies. I still see your pictures on the late show. You were a
marvelous actor.
                              ED
Thank you.
                         MR. WARREN
...I mean, the Odets plays, Broadway...You were really good.

                              ED
Yes, wasn't I?
                         MR. WARREN
Whatever happened to you?

                              ED
I died, didn't you hear?

MR. WARREN
(Hesitates, then laughs)
Ha-ha, very good. No, really, where've you been?

ED
Well, really, I was called out to head up the film industry in
Mongolia.
MR. WARREN
(Thinks HE's being put on, but not sure)
What? Mongolia?

ED
Well, it's a small industry, but it's growing. We just put out our
first picture. It's called "Mongolian Idiots."

MR. WARREN
(Coolly)
Um-hmm. Well, if you don't want to tell me.
ED
I've been blacklisted.
MR. WARREN
Ah, right, right, the political thing. I knew you' gone wrong
somewhere. Now I remember. You came out for Russia.

ED
No, no, I never...
MR. WARREN
That's bad business. What did you want to get involved in that
stuff for? Leave the thinking to the thinkers. You stay out of
trouble and make your bucks.

ED
Actually, I was in it for the broads.
MR. WARREN
The women, that's worse.

ED
(Doing a character)

How was I to know? Some guy mentions the Communist Party, I think he's talkin' about someplace with drinks and girls! So, I get there and all these people are talkin' about Russia and Negroes and I don't know what they're talkin' about. And pretty soon this guys asks me if I would steal some military secrets from Paramount Pictures, and I tell him, "There ain't no military secrets at Paramount Pictures! They're all over at Warner Brothers!"

MR. WARREN

You think you're pretty funny, don't you.

ED

Maybe we'll call the picture "Mr. Warren and the Mongolian Idiots."

MR. WARREN

You be as clever as you like, fella, 'cause you deserve everything you get.

ED

Yes, well I think you're eminently qualified to lecture me on the conduct of my life. After all, a man of your outstanding achievements in art and the world...

MR. WARREN

Oh, brother, when you big guys fall, you really show your true colors.

(The inner door opens)

GRACE

Mr. Warren, please.

ED

(Jumps up)

Now you wait one minute!

MR. WARREN
(Trying to get by ED)

Excuse me, please!

ED

I was here before this man!

MR. WARREN
(Shoves ED aside, at door)

I hope you never work again!
(HE exits)

ED

He did not have an appointment!

GRACE

I'm very sorry, Mr. Morris. I'm only doing what I'm told!

ED
(Trying to look beyond her into a third inner
office)

Is he in there? Is Jack Stone in there? Did you tell him I'm out
here?

GRACE

I told his assistant, Mr. Ober...

ED

What did he say?

GRACE

He didn't say anything...

ED

He must have said something! Did he tell Mr. Stone that I'm
here?!

GRACE

I don't know...

ED

Then Mr. Stone <u>is</u> in there!

GRACE

I...No, he's not...

ED

Then who are these people going in to see?!

GRACE

Mr. Morris, I was told to tell you that Mr. Stone is not in the office, and could-you-call-again-in-the-near-future!

ED

Now, look, dear, he's in there and you can get to him...

GRACE

Mr. Morris, please...

ED

No, I'm asking your help...

GRACE

Mr. Morris, I'm going to have to close this door...

ED

I'm going in there!
                    (HE crosses into inner office)

GRACE

The next door is locked! Will you leave, Mr. Morris, or do I call the police?

ED

                    (From inner office)
Jack! It's me, Ed Morris! I just want to talk to you! I don't care if you have nothing for me! But we were friends!

GRACE'S VOICE

Operator, get me the police...

ED

Friends! You were at my house! We worked together! ...

GRACE

I'd like an officer sent to...

ED

Doesn't that mean anything to you?!

GRACE

55 East 60th Street, suite…

ED

Never mind, I'm leaving!
          (ED crosses to outer office,Still calling out. Door to
Inner office slams)
Then how about this? I made money for you! You made money on
my name! Money, you made money, and now for money you don't
know me! What kind of man does that make you?! What kind of
man forsakes his friend for coin?
          (HE stands there raging to the closed door)
Talk-to-me!
          (Silence. HE exits office, slamming door behind him.)

          LIGHTS: Out on office and come up on
          apartment.

ED

          (ED paces in the bedroom while COOKIE dresses)
…And I ended up shouting out in the outer office. Suggesting he
was a Judas. Stupid! Stupid!

COOKIE

Yes, it was.

ED

I said it was! I'll go back. No, that's no good…I'll call. I'll speak to
Grace. She seems like a nice girl. I'll apologize, ask her to convey
my apologies to him. Just know that if only I could talk to him,
convince him that he's big enough to break this thing. I don't
want to lead, just a small part, but one that will show people that
someone is standing up, someone's not afraid…
          (HE stops, notices how SHE's dressing)
Why are you dressing like that?

                    COOKIE
What?
                    ED
Why are you dressing like that?
                    COOKIE
Like what?

                    ED
In old clothes. It's not what you wear to work.
                    COOKIE
Well…

                    ED
It's not your housecleaning clothes…

                    COOKIE
No…
                    ED
Why are you dressing like that?

                    COOKIE
I'm…going to see someone…who's not doing too well. I don't
want to shame her.
                    ED
Don't lie to me! Why are you wearing old clothes?

                    COOKIE
These aren't so old. I think look rather well…

                    ED
Cookie! Don't hide things from me! Tell me!

                    COOKIE
I…
                    ED
No lies!

COOKIE

Alright, I'll tell you. I'm going to see a woman I know. To borrow money.

(Sighs)

You're an actor on the stage. I'm an actress in the world. I play the part of a woman who goes to borrow money. I'm very good at it. I could instruct you in it.

(Speaks into mirror)

If you want to borrow money that will never be repaid, you must wear a threadbare suit. Elegant kid gloves, but old, with a bit of finger showing through. Very little powder on the face. A shiny
forehead says trouble. As you wait at her door, rub your eyes till they're red, the suggestion of a teary scene at home. The important thing through it all is to think of your beautiful children. How they smile, how they sing. How they bring in the sunlight to your husband's dark world.

ED

(To audience)

What can I say to her? Things will be better? It's been said so often in this house, it's become cheap currency.

COOKIE

Be dignified as you relate the story of your husband's troubles. And when your well-to-do friend (who you remember still as an avaricious secretary) begins to cluck her tongue, resist, on pain of starvation, the urge to smash her in the face. Again, think of your beautiful children.

ED

How long have you been doing this?

COOKIE

Oh, a year or so.

ED

No more. Don't go anymore.

COOKIE

I don't mind it. It's a lesson in human relations.

ED

Don't go.

COOKIE

You haven't let me finish. Don't expect the interview to last long. Don't expect to be given coffee. That's for current and already conquered friends. Certainly not a drink. That's for current but not yet conquered friends. Not a single glass of water. You're not the delivery boy. You'll be offered a frozen smile on a silver platter. That's alright, you just keep thinking of your beautiful children.

ED

(To audience)

There are times when a woman has stored up her humiliations, when she wants to give some back to you. She doesn't want you to do anything. Just stand there and take it.

COOKIE

You should practice at home the woman's art of staring out French windows into the night for endless length of time she keeps you standing by her desk, as she writes out the check. If you can stare long enough without breaking, you'll find you're making up to one hundred dollars a visit. You leave graciously with ice on your heart.

ED

(To audience)

But you must do something.

COOKIE

Oh, yes, on your way home, in the subway station, after you straighten up, check your coat for spots of vomit. Keep thinking of the children.

(A moment of silence)

ED

You must be very angry with me.

COOKIE

I don't want to be.

ED

Things will be better.

COOKIE

Of course.

ED

(A pause, then)

I love you, Cookie.

COOKIE

I know.

(SHE rises, smiles at him)

You know it's dawned on me after all these years of thinking I was a revolutionary, I'm a thoroughly middle class woman. My status is declining, and I'm violated. Silly, isn't it.

ED

No, not at all.

COOKIE

(Starts for door)

I have to go.

ED

You know what?

(SHE stops)

That insurance job Al offered. I think I'll take it. It'll give me something to do. Just until I straighten things out with Stone.

COOKIE

(Gently)

Not for me, Ed. Don't do it for me.

ED

No, for me. I need activity, get a different view of things.

COOKIE

Alright, if you want.

ED

I'll call Al now.

LIGHTS:Fade to

BLACKOUT

LIGHTS:Up on dining area.

(Late at night. ED and AL, a Balding man in his fifties, sit
At the table, a bottle of ScotchAnd glasses between them. As the Lights come up, we hear them singing the last crooning phrases of a song)

BOTH

"Rozshinkas mit mandlen,
Shlof, mein kindele, shlof,
Rozshinkas mit mandlen
Schlof, mein kindele, shlof."

(They fall into a warm silence.ED pours the whiskey straight into their tumblers. THEY drink silently.)

AL

Do you remember the old country at all?

ED

No, I was only three when we left.

AL

I remember a railroad station somewhere in Poland. I was just learning to read, and I got fascinated by this sign. It took a little work to figure it out.

                    ED
What did it say?

                    AL
"Men's room."

                    ED
"Men's room?" That's all?

                    AL
Yeah, "Men's room."

                    ED
That's your cherished memory of the old country?

                    AL
It's all I remember. Whattayou want?

                    ED
It's a lousy memory.

                    AL
It's better than you! You don't remember anything at all!

                    ED
I'd rather not, if the best I can come up with is "Men's Room"! For
Christ's sake, Al, you could make up a better one than that!

                    AL
Why should I? It's what I remember. Leave it be.

                    ED
I mean, the ocean voyage was stormy and all of us huddled together
in steerage, and my mother sang us songs to calm us. Now that's
something worth remembering. The thundering seas, the vessel
pitching dangerously, and your mother with her arms around all of
you singing gently but bravely into the teeth of the storm.

                    AL
Yeah, well firstly, my mother could never get her arms around all
of us, because there were seven of us. And secondly, she couldn't
carry a tune with a shovel. And thirdly, it didn't happen that way.

ED

How do you know? All you remember is the men's room. For all you know you may be the survivor of a great shipwreck.

AL

Oh, come on! Something like that I would remember, definitely.

ED

Not necessarily! Some terrible things that have happened to me I don't remember.

AL

Yeah? Like what?

ED

(Thinks, then)
I don't remember.
(THEY look at each other and burst out into loud laughter at the idiocy of the conversation. Then ED motions for AL to quiet down.)
Shhh! Shh! Don't want to wake Cookie. Your sister has a fine temper when you bother her sleep.
(THEY again subside into silence. AL looks at ED queerly for a long moment)
What is it? What're you looking at?

AL

You.

ED

Why? What's wrong?

AL

Nothing. Just thinking.

ED

Thinking what?

AL

Every so often I think about it, and I remember.

                              ED
Remember what?

                              AL
                       (Incredulously)
You're a movie star. My sister married a movie star. Just now I
looked at you and thought, Jesus Christ, I'm sitting here drinking
Scotch with a movie star, like we're friends, like a dream.

                              ED
We are friends.

                              AL
But what I'm saying is that you're a movie star.

                              ED
                          (Sighs)
Fine, alright, but don't say it anymore, please.

                              AL
Oh, Ed, I'm sorry. I didn't mean it to remind you of…

                              ED
No, no, it's alright. It's just that I don't often think of those
days. When I think of Hollywood, all I can remember is "Men's
Room."

                              AL
I understand. Still, to climb as high as you did was something.
                       (A pause)
You'll be back. You wait. You'll see.

                              ED
                   (Almost to himself)
I love this country.
                       (To AL)
I love this country. Can you understand that?

                              AL

Well, yeah,

              (ED studies him for a long moment, then)

                              ED

Al? What would you have done?

                              AL

When?

                              ED

Before the committee?

                              AL

You mean testifying?

                              ED

Yes. Which way would you have gone?

                              AL

Well...I don't know...I, uh...

                              ED

Come on, level with me.

                              AL

Well, I'm not political...

                              ED

You're alive, so you must have an opinion. Tell me.

                              AL

Well...to be honest, at the time...I thought you were crazy.

                              ED

And now?

                              AL

              (Struggling to comprehend something)

Ed, why? Why did you do it? You were up there with the gods.
You had a fine home, and famous people came to visit you.
You were known everywhere. I mean, I was famous in my
neighborhood for being your brother-in-law! And just that little
taste of fame was so delicious to me, what must it have been like

up there where you were. You were the dream, the immigrant kid who walked off the boat and became a movie star. You had it all right here in your hand, and you let it go. Why? For Communism? For the Constitution? Those are words. I can't believe that's why you did it?

ED

No.

AL

Then why?

ED

Well...At first it was like being in a very heroic movie, and we were the stars. Everyone applauded us wherever we went. But then when they sent the first bunch to jail, real jail, it go to be serious. When my time came I did think a lot about the Constitution. It did protect the people, so it needed protection. So, I went down there and did my piece. Even then people were saying, "Well, they can't touch you, Ed. You're a star. Those guys they sent away were writers and such, intellectuals. Who knew them? But you? They can't touch you." Then, to everyone's astonishment and surprise, they touched me. And no one was more surprised than Edward Morris. Then for a while I persisted because the idea of stoolpigeoning repelled me. There's something instinctual in the race that is repulsed by the notion of selling one's brother. Of course, here it's the law of the wolf. And all they're asking of me is that I obey the law and be a little wolfish. One short, wolfy hour on the stand and they'll let me go about my business. Not a big request.

AL

It's not! Everybody does it!

ED

Yes, I know. Then why can't I?

AL

That's what I'm asking you!

ED

And I'm saying I don't know. But let me ask you this? Who are those men who ask this of me? Are they paragons? Are they solons? Are they the wise men of our tribe? Or are they grafters and schemers and liars and murderers?! Is it before such men I have to spend my little hour in the dust?!

AL

Yes! Just like the rest of us!
			(Lights come up on the wintry street. KIEHL in overcoat stands and addresses ED, while AL freezes.)

KIEHL

It was very simple for your friend, Charles Allman.

ED
			(Answers from where HE is.)
My ex-friend.

KIEHL

He still speaks well of you.

ED

He spoke well of me to the Committee.

KIEHL

We needed your name.

ED

We?

KIEHL
			(Smiles, having been caught)
I meant the Committee.

ED

I'm sure you did. Did Charlie have to crawl when he recanted?

KIEHL

Very little. That's the point of having me handle it. I'm your friend at court. I insure discretion.

                              ED
And if I reject your offer?

                            KIEHL
Things will get worse.

                              ED
I see. A war of attrition.

                            KIEHL
We're in no hurry.

                              ED
                   (Studies KIEHL)
Mr. Kiehl, what would you do if you had state power?

                            KIEHL
                   (Coldly)
I'd put a gun to your head and give you sixty seconds.

                              ED
And without the gun?

                            KIEHL
The tactic is simple. Cut the beast from the herd, turn the herd
against him, and the heard will destroy him.

                              ED
You mean the people?

                            KIEHL
I mean your own family.
                   (Lights fade on KIEHL and street.AL unfreezes)

                              ED
                   (gesturing to where KIEHL had been)
And be led to the dust pit by a madman? This man Kiehl is mad!
Life to him is the continuing horror of a conspiracy! His only
relief is in world suicide! Am I to adopt his attitude of despair?! Is
that the legacy I'm to pass down to my children?!

AL

Is it better for you to be destroyed and them dragged with you?!

ED

I don't know! I'm fighting like hell to prevent it! I don't know what's going to happen! But I know this: the power has gone mad! To continue to grovel before it is to insure an insane world for our children!

(COOKIE, in nightgown, stands in the doorway)

COOKIE

You woke me up.

BLACKOUT

<u>CURTAIN</u>

<u>END OF ACT I</u>

ACT II
PROLOGUE

(ED comes out in street clothes,Goes to a small make-up mirrorHanging on a rack, applies eye Shadow to darken under his eyes.As HE does so, to audience.)

ED

I'll sing you a song. Here's one, short.
(HE sings)
You are so you,
Under grey skies or blue,
The you-ness of you,
Will always come through,
Because God made a mistake
And forgot to make someone else—youuuu.
(HE finishes with make-up,starts off, stops, to audience, cheerfully.)
By the way, things are getting worse.
(HE does his flourish, bow.)
Para-pa-ti, para-pa-tu!
(HE walks into living room.)

ACT II

LIGHTS UP ON: Living room area.

ED

(On the phone. JOE,hidden in the hallway,listens secretly.)

ED(CONT'D)

I start tomorrow. Selling insurance...No, no, I'm looking forward
to it. It's a challenge. A depressing challenge, but a challenge
nevertheless. The theory is that they may be too frightened to
hire me as an actor but guilty enough to buy my policy...What are
you doing this morning? ... I thought I might drop over. Not for
long...I need to see you...In about twenty minutes...You can wear
whatever you like...

I'll be the fellow in the black derby hat...that's right, just like in
the dirty movies, black stockings and garter belt.
                (HE laughs heartily)
Yes, it feels good to laugh...What? "Morning Madness"? Yes, that's
a good title for it...You're a sweet girl...Yours truly, "Expectant."
                (HE hangs up. JOE enters from the shadows with
FRANZ)

                        JOE
Dad? Would you like to go for a walk?

                        ED
Well, I have an appointment downtown.

                        JOE
I'll walk you part way.
                        ED
                (Gestures to FRANZ)
Are you going to bring him?

                        JOE
I usually do. He'll be quiet.

                        ED
Alright, let's go.

ED(CONT'D)
LIGHTS: change from room lights to
autumn daylight.

A tree lined street. Green and yellow fills the stage, as the fall sun filters through the branches onto the WALKERS.

JOE
(Looking behind him)
They're following us.

ED
(In his thoughts)
What?

JOE
In the car. The two men.

ED
(looks behind him)
Oh, yes. Always.
(THEY walk around the stage as if going from block to block.)
Oh, God, that gave us the winds of autumn! God's perfume, Joe!
(HE whirls around with pleasure,then remembers the MEN in the car, resumes walking)

JOE
(After a moment)
Do you believe in God?

ED
No.

JOE
Then why do you use his name?

ED
(Doesn't answer, then)
Man is God, Joe. I am. You are.

                            JOE

And Stone?

                            ED

The bastard! Yes, he definitely is! Man and nature, that's God. The
church, just another real estate company. You wait, the people
are going to take this earth yet.

                            JOE

I believe in God.

                            ED
                    (Swallows, then)
Alright. That's your right.
                    (THEY walk in silence,turn corner into a stiff wind,
heads
down again THEY go through it,then it lets up.)
Why?

                            JOE

Why what?

                            ED

Why do you believe in God?

                            JOE

Well...
                    (THEY walk a few more steps,then JOE stops.)
Well, I don't know. I just believe there must be some force greater
than man.

                            ED

Well, I said, nature!

                            JOE

Greater than that

                            ED

What, old greybeard in the sky?! When you think of all the starving
people in the world handing in their pennies to some church
because they're hooked on that lie! When you think of that, and all
that I've taught you, and then you come out and say that! ...
                    (HE stalks off. JOE chases after)

JOE
(Lamely)
I have a right to my beliefs.

ED
(Stops, turn on him, gestures behind toward the
TWO MEN.)
Why the hell do you think I opposed the Committee?! Because
they're God-playing! My God, Joe, if you don't understand that...!
(HE walks a distance further,stops.)
When I was in the orphan home, we were only allowed to
speak
when our number was called. If we spoke out of turn, we were
punished. You know how? The other boys took off a shoe and
gave us as many whacks as were in our number. My number was
twenty-seven. Out of a class of thirty! No, there is no Goddam
God! There are only men! They make their choices and live them
out!
(Walks another distance, stops)
And I'll tell you something else. As long as you believe in God,
you'll be a victim!
(Shoves his fist to heaven)
I bow my head to no man!
(ED sees he has intimidated his son.)
I didn't mean to shout at you. I'm a little edgy this morning. You
believe whatever you want.

JOE
Well, I'm no fanatic about it. I mean, maybe there isn't a God. I
don't know. All I'm saying, I guess, is I don't know.
(ED looks at his SON, defeated by his victory. HE starts
walking again, stops, waits for JOE to catch up with him. THEY
walksilently together.As THEY walk, JOE suddenly laughs.)
Do you remember that time when I was nine when you chased
me through the house?

ED

I did? No, I don't remember.

JOE

Boy, it was a riot. I yelled at Mom, I think, and you heard it out in the garden. I saw you through the window. I didn't bother to wait for you. I started running. We ran all over that house, upstairs and downstairs, inside and out. Finally you caught me in the upstairs hallway.

ED

And?

JOE

And what?

ED

And what happened?

FRANZ

You choked him unconscious! Hee-hee!

ED

(To JOE, stopping the walk to face him.)
What? I don't remember that! Is it true?

JOE

Golly, Dad, I don't remember.

FRANZ

The king put down the uprising!

ED

Joe, is that how you feel? Is that what you think I do to you?

JOE

Oh, heck, no, Dad. That's just him big-mouthing...

ED

Then why did you bring up that story?

                                   JOE
It struck my mind. I thought it was funny, us running through the
halls.

                                   ED
                   (Looks deep in his SON's eyes,then)
Joe, if there's anything you've got to say to me, I wish you'd trust
me enough to say it directly.

                                   JOE
Absolutely, I will. If there's anything...
                        (Again THEY walk silently.)

                                   ED
I don't know what I'd do without you, Joe. You're my right arm.
                                   JOE
                        (Thrilled, but just shrugs)
Oh, hell...

                                   ED
No, you are.
                                   JOE
                   (Studies the sidewalk as they walk.)
I don't do anything.
                                   ED
You do. Aside from bringing in money. Well, you keep me
company when I need it.
                        (HE stops again, JOE too)
This thing about your mother crying at night. I appreciate your
going in to her. To comfort her.
                   (HE stops, puts his hand on JOE's arm)
I know what you're thinking. It should be me in there. Well,
maybe. But sometimes the husband's presence aggravates
things...A lot of it I know is this trouble she's had, but also the
stress and strain of the past few years. Christ, you know, one of
the most difficult things in this kind of situation is to separate the
events of your inner world from those of your outer. I don't know
what to blame.

ED(CONT'D)
(Shrugs off his confusion, starts walking again)
Look, I promise you, things are going to get better soon. I know
it. I'm going to get through to Stone. Then you watch the change
in your mother.
(HE stops again, nods toward building.)
Well, this is where I go.

JOE
(Looks up)
Your appointment's here?

ED
Yes, a writer I know.

JOE
(Looks deep into his FATHER's eyes)
Don't go up there, Dad.

ED
(Struck, but feigning innocence)
What do you mean?

JOE
I know where you're going.
(ED doesn't respond)
I know who's up there.

ED
Who is up there? Sounds interesting.

JOE
A woman.

ED
(The mask falls off)
How do you know?

JOE
I know.

ED
(Thinks, studies the BOY, then)
This has nothing to do with your mother. I love her.

JOE

Then why do you come here?

ED

Because...because...If I was working, I wouldn't come here.

JOE

What? That doesn't mean anything.

ED

No, I guess it doesn't, to you.

JOE

Come on, let's walk some more.

ED

No. Joe, listen to me. This isn't something I'm proud of. It's something I need. It has to do with growing older. It has to do with loss.

JOE

Loss? Of what?

ED

Of...a lot of things! Dammit, why do you have to press me like this?!

JOE

You said it, "The family united."

ED

We are!

JOE

Then why this?!

ED

I said, this has nothing to do with us!

JOE

It does! You're cheating!

ED

No! I need relief! I need new dreams! Conquests!
                    (Gestures the BOY away.)
Joe! Don't press me!
                    (HE rushes up the stairs, disappearing.)

JOE

                    (Takes FRANZ from under his arm, props him up.)
Franz, what do you want to be when you grow up?

FRANZ

I want to be a political martyr.

JOE

Why do you want to be that?

FRANZ

So, when I get in trouble with my family, I can visit young lady
writers in fifth floor walk-ups.
                    JOE

Really? Won't you feel guilty?

FRANZ

A little when I enter her building, but then with my bad heart each
flight will give me pain. By the time I reach the fifth floor I will
have done penance. By the time I enter her door I will be absolved.
And by the time I enter her I will be "Saint Franz of the Blacklist."

BLACKOUT

(In the blackout)

SECRETARY'S VOICE

Mr. Morris, wanted in the outer office. Mr. Morris, come to the
outer office.

LIGHTS UP ON:The outer office of AL's insurance
agency.

(KIEHLsits on a lounge chair. CHARLIE ALLMAN,
dressed in flamboyant red,Gold, and brown corduroys, paces
The cramped space. HE is tanned, Sleek, athletic looking, in his
forties.)

CHARLIE

We go back a long way. His son, Joseph, is named after my father.

KIEHL

Is that so.

CHARLIE

He was best man at my wedding. Twice. . I drove Cookie to the
hospital when Joseph was born. Ed was onstage at the time, I think.
Yes, he was working. I saw her through practically the whole delivery.

KIEHL

Mr. Allman, you're wearing a rut in the floor.

CHARLIE

Why does it have to be here? I'd really rather it was at my house.

KIEHL

Would he come to your house?

CHARLIE

(Stops, to KIEHL)

Respect is the key word here. There must be great respect.

KIEHL

I respect him. Just tell him your idea.

CHARLIE

Wait a minute now, Kiehl. It was your idea.

KIEHL

Alright, mine. You just present it.

    (CHARLIE starts to pace again asED enters. HE
sees the TWO MENand stops. Ignoring KIEHL, HE Takes in his
OLD FRIEND. CHARLIE turns to him and studies him in his
White shirt and tie. ED, awareNow of his business dress, is
Embarrassed. ALL THREE seem petrified for a moment. CHARLIE
Breaks the ice by rushing up to ED and embracing him. ED, not
knowing what to do, lets him.)

CHARLIE

Ed, Christ, ED, how are you? My God, how well you look! I've
thought of calling you so many times! But, you know, I've been
bouncing around so much, Europe, the Coast...! It really is good
to see you! How's Cookie?

ED

(Gently pushing Charlie away)

She's fine.

CHARLIE

The kids?

ED

Fine.

CHARLIE

Wonderful! That's just...!

ED

(To KIEHL)

Why did you bring him here?

CHARLIE

I want to see you, Ed! Renew old times...!

ED

(To KIEHL)

Why?

KIEHL

Mr. Allman has an idea he wants to talk over with you.

ED

Why here?!

CHARLIE

You're right, Ed, this isn't a good place. Why don't you and the family come to my place tomorrow night. We'll have a big roast, a feast, and you and I will take a bottle into the library and put on some music and have a long discussion...

KIEHL

I suggest you start it here, Mr. Allman.

CHARLIE

I know how Ed loves the library in my apartment. He said it, "I like a room with high ceilings and wood paneling."

KIEHL

We're all here now, Mr. Allman.

CHARLIE

I'm not blind, Mr. Kiehl! I see we're all here.

ED

(To KIEHL)
Excuse me, I have work to do.
(HE starts to exit)

CHARLIE

Ed, wait!
(ED stops)
I want to talk to you.
(ED waits)
I just wrote a picture. I'm producing it myself. You're perfect for the lead.

ED

You look like an artist, Charlie.

CHARLIE

You look fine, yourself, Ed.

ED

Yes. It's my insurance costume.

CHARLIE

Would you like to read the script?

ED

I don't think so.

CHARLIE

Why not? What can it hurt?

ED

I'm afraid I'd find Mr. Kiehl in it somewhere.

(CHARLIE takes ED aside.SOTTO voce)

CHARLIE

Ed, what the hell are a couple of names? You get in and get out
and forget it. Look, three names. You name Phil who it can't hurt
because he's dead. Me, who it can't hurt, because I'm cleared
already. And for the new name give 'em Bob Coles, because he's
in England and it can't hurt him. They'll settle for those three.

ED

How is your sleeping, Charlie? Do you sleep well?

CHARLIE

Yes, fine. Listen...

ED

I'm not. I've developed insomnia. My mind goes all night.

CHARLIE

Ed, you've got to ride over these little men. Let them play their little game. It doesn't mean anything.

ED

And you appetite, is it good?

CHARLIE

Fine, I'm eating fine. Ed, it's an hour out of your life…

ED

I've got a nervous stomach. Isn't that funny? You'd think taking a principal position would give you peace of mind.

CHARLIE

Ed, that's the point. It doesn't matter what's happened up to now. We've got to get you working again. You should be working.

ED

Yes, I should.

CHARLIE

Then let Kiehl set it up. The only public part is the press conference. And that's fine minutes of double-talk and then you go home. I swear to you, there's nothing to it. Then you're clear.

ED

I see.

CHARLIE

I've missed you Eduardo. I'm looking forward to working with you. We're shooting the picture in London. You love London, I know that.

ED

Yes, I do.

CHARLIE

Then what do you say? Will you talk to Kiehl?

ED
(Studies his OLD FRIEND)

Charlie, do you mean you never had any bad feelings about naming me?

CHARLIE

Eddie, I assumed you'd play the game.

ED

You didn't assume it the first time you went.

CHARLIE

What the hell did I know then? I was playing a part. Being heroic. Then I saw it was this game where I name you, you name so-and-so, he names another, and so on, until these little creeps fritter their way into history, and you and I go on. Free to do our work.

ED

Free,
                    (Moves toward KIEHL)
Charlie, what is your relationship to this man?

CHARLIE

What do you mean?

ED

Is he your friend?

CHARLIE

Well, he's been very helpful...

ED

Is he a colleague?

CHARLIE

No, he's not an...

ED

Well, describe the relationship. Give it a name.

ED

Let me put it to you this way. Do you call him and he shows up, or does he call you and you show up?

CHARLIE
(Caught, then)

I don't see where that has any bearing on what we're talking about, Ed.

ED

Don't you remember about the artist and history, Charlie? No matter which way you and I go, Kiehl wins. So we might as well go our own way.

CHARLIE

Still full of brave speeches, huh, pal? Well, speak on. I've had enough.
(HE heads for exit, stops)
As long as you have that attitude, you deserve to sell insurance!
(HE exits. KIEHL gets up and briskly goes to the reception window.)

KIEHL

I'd like to see Mr. Albert Goodman. Mr. Richard Kiehl is calling.

ED
(Crosses to KIEHL)

What do you want with him?

KIEHL

(Turns on ED)

Mr. Goodman, are you aware that you have in your employ a man who has a long record of subversive activities? A man who has contemptuously defied a committee of the Congress of the United States? A man who has hidden his seditious beliefs behind the fifth amendment to the Constitution like any common criminal?

ED

You dog...

KIEHL

Do you think it right that you employ such a man? Would your clients think it right?

ED

You remorseless dog...

KIEHL

While American boys are dying in Korea, you're giving aid and comfort to a man, who, by his own avowals, has sided with the enemy!

(It all rises in ED. HE lashes out, striking KIEHL in the face
and knocking him down.)

ED

Bastard! Get up! Get up!

BLACKOUT

(In the blackout)

COOKIE'S VOICE

Sabotage!

ED'S VOICE

No, he pushed me to it!

COOKIE'S VOICE

You hated it, so you sabotaged it!

ED'S VOICE

No, I was doing well!

COOKIE'S VOICE

You hit him! The girl saw it!

ED'S VOICE

I didn't mean to!

LIGHTS: up.

ED and COOKIE in their bedroom. HE is dressed in his own
clothes now,not the business clothes.

COOKIE

You did! You wanted out!

ED

No, he brought Charlie in! I couldn't stand seeing Charlie! Then
he started saying things, and I just blew!

COOKIE

You just blew! And now he's suing us!

ED

Let him! The stinking bastard! I want a day in court! I want my
side heard!

COOKIE

Your side?! Your side is the side of a temperamental child!
Someone says something and you hit them!

ED

No! He provoked me! He wanted me to hit him!

COOKIE

And you did!

ED

Yes, Goddammit, I did! I'm a man!

COOKIE

You're also the head of a family!

ED

(Controls himself, trying to be calm and reasonable)
Cookie, the man was there to get me fired…

COOKIE

(Also toning down)
And you played right into his hands.

ED

Maybe I did but not intentionally.

COOKIE

Not consciously, no.

ED

What do you mean, consciously?

COOKIE

Ed, you didn't want that job.

ED

I did!

COOKIE

No. It violated you, having to be like the rest of us, and you took this way out.

ED

No! He was going to threaten Al politically!

COOKIE

That's what you say.

ED

It's what he said!

COOKIE

Then why didn't the receptionist mention it?!

ED

I don't know! She was there! She heard it! I guess she got frightened!

COOKIE

The political thing!

ED

Now wait a minute. If a person hears something, they hear it. It has nothing to do with the political thing.

COOKIE

But it does!Ed, you can't hide everything behind the political hysteria! You can't always be a martyr!

ED

I'm not trying to be!

COOKIE

I'm sure you're not, consciously...Look, Ed, I support you in your fight. But at times I feel you use it, exploit it.

ED

Cookie, listen to what you're saying. It's what they want you to say. To have us at each other's throats.

COOKIE

That's what I mean. In your mind everything is them. If I contradict you, it's them speaking...

ED

I didn't say that...

COOKIE

If you something wrong, and someone points it out, it's them attacking...

ED

Remember the tactic...

COOKIE

I know the tactic!

ED

...Cut the beast from the herd...

COOKIE

...Turn the herd against him...

ED

....And the herd will destroy him! We must fight against that! We're all ragged. I know that. You think I can't smell the suppressed feelings in this place? Franz gets ruder all the time! That poor girl is in there painting herself into a frenzy! You! I see it in you! But we've got to hold on! Don't let it break until I break through!

(SHE coldly turns and starts out.)

Where are you going? I'm talking to you!

COOKIE

(Stops, turns to him)

I'm tired of your lectures. When you start making money again, I'll listen.

(SHE exits, leaving him stunned.)

BLACKOUT

The stage is dark.

ED'S VOICE ON THE PHONE

Listen, goddam it, you said he'd be in today! You said it, you! Don't lie to me...! No, I'm not accusing you, but you said he'd talk to me today! ... Lies!

LIGHTS:Up .

ED

(on the phone wearing a red robe over his Balzac costume.)

No, don't hang up! I lost my temper, forgive me. Listen, Grace. You and I have gotten to know each other over these last few months, so I think I can be quite candid with you. Now, I'm not simply talking about a man being turned against by his family. It's far bigger than

that. It's war they want! It's cruel massive war the God-men are creating! Russia in flames! China in flames! Even at the risk of this country in flames! And all those who oppose it condemned to silence!

(JOE walks through the room withFRANZ, stops, regards ED for a moment, then exits back to his room. ED stops talking for a moment,HE and his SON's eyes meet.

when the BOY has left, HE resumes in a lowered voice, more urgently.)

...No, wait! I'm telling you this for a reason! ... Do you have children? ... How old? ... For them, then, to spare them. Children must not suffer for our crimes! That's why, for your children and mine, I'm asking you to look deep in your soul, please, and despite his wishes, give me a chance to talk to Stone, to break the silence before it goes too far!

(COOKIE enters and looks at ED, who smiles at her, as HE waits for Grace to decide)

COOKIE

(Coldly)

I'm going to the store.

(SHE exits)

ED

What? Yes? You will?! Thank you! Thank you, dear! Putting me through! Christ, a chance! One chance!

      (STONE's voice comes on the other end of the phone. ED is struck dumb. STONE repeats his hellos.)

STONE'S VOICE

Hello? Hello? Anyone there? ... No one there.

(ED's mouth moves but no words come out. Again STONE speaks, but ED is silent, his free hand clutching his throat, rubbing it desperately to free his chokingvoice. Finally STONE clicks off.At last, into the dead line, ED blurts out.)

ED

John! John?! Too late!

      (HE collapses to his knees, sighs)

I couldn't speak. The silence is in me now.

      (ED stands, hangs up phone.TERRY enters from her room in a filthy smock. SHE is dragging with fatigue)

Why aren't you dressing?

TERRY

I have no dress.

ED

I thought you bought one yesterday.

TERRY

No.

ED

You said you were going out.

TERRY

I didn't.

ED

Why not?

TERRY

It's all too much!
                    (In a driven but exhausted tone)
To choose a dress, to buy a candy bar, to walk through crowds, or
see the janitor! It's all to much!

ED
                    (Crosses to her, takes her hand)
Dearest, why? What is it?

TERRY

They all want from me!
                              ED

Want? What?

TERRY

Space, space! And all from me!
                    (HE is near her. SHE smells his fragrance)
The odor of tobacco pursues me! Bay rum urges me on, points
out mistakes, watches me fall, drives me on, paint out his eyes!

ED
                    (embraces her)
No, sweetheart, I don't want you to!

TERRY

I want to!
                              ED
Terry, I saw the last one of him you did. The eyes had no power.

TERRY
                    (Sighs)
It's sweet of you to say, but I know it's not so. He still resists. His
green eyes are too much!

ED

Let it go.
            (Tries to pull her up)
Come, let's tear up the paintings.

TERRY

No!
            (Then more calmly)
Not that way. I'm going to kill him. Cut out his manhood! But my way! Paint out his eyes!

ED
            (Sees her obsessive fury)
Terry, what is it?

TERRY

What?

ED

What's wrong?

TERRY

Nothing, why?

ED

No, look in your eyes. Has something happened? Tell me.

TERRY

Nothing.
            (SHE starts back to her room)
I have to get back to work.

ED
            (Blocks her way)
You're hiding something! Is it me?

TERRY

No!

ED
(Grabs her by shoulders)
Tell me! About Kiehl?!

TERRY
(Shrieks)
No!

ED
Yes! Now tell me!

TERRY
(Bursts into sobs, collapses In chai.r)
It's terrible! Terrible! I don't know how he got in!

ED
Got in? Into the house?

TERRY
I didn't let him in! Kill me if I did! But suddenly there he was! But
I didn't tell him anything! No matter all the tricks he tried! This
time I wasn't fooled! ...

ED
Wait! Wait, now. Calm down. Tell me slowly, from the beginning.
What happened?

TERRY
The other day I was alone in the apartment working. I began to
think about your battle with the Committee. I got upset. So bad
that I got a spell of nausea. So I went into the bathroom. At first I
was doing it into the bowl, I felt a hand pressing my brow. At first I
thought it was you, that you'd come home and heard me, so I let him
go until I was finished. But then when I stood up, I saw it was him...!

ED
Kiehl? ...

TERRY

I started to scream, but he put his hand over my mouth! He said if I made any sound he'd kill me.

(ED's breathing starts to become a wheeze)

He took me back in my room and told me to lay down on the bed. I was terrified he'd see the painting, 'cause then I knew he'd kill me, but he didn't even look over there. He just lay down next to me and started rubbing me in places and talking to me in that soft tone of voice…

ED

What did he say?

TERRY

Oh, nothing that would sound bad. That's how clever he is. Just about things and places. About some countryside he used to travel and seaports with green waves against a breakwater. I was so frightened I can't remember it all. He said he wanted to take me to Denmark. He said the winter sun of Denmark can calm the most disturbed woman in the world. I knew he was trying to get me to say something then, like "I'm not disturbed" or something, but I didn't want to let him, but I was frightened. And also I thought, maybe this is another trick, thinking he can get me to say something that way. Well, I let him do what he wanted. I lay there silent as a stone.

ED

(Carefully)

Teresa, listen to me. I think you may have imagined this.

TERRY

No, he really came in…

ED

Well, dreamed it then. A very strong dream tied to your work… There are two locks on the door. There was no way he could get in.

TERRY

Are you serious? They can get in anytime they want! They have keys for everything!

ED

No, they don't, dear...

TERRY

Are you saying I let him in? I'm your only defender around here! How can you think that of me?! Oh, I see! You still blame me for the other time! ...

ED

I don't!

TERRY

You do! You think I want to betray you!

ED

No!

TERRY

What do I have to do to prove I'm loyal?! All my life I've proved it! At school and here and in my work, and then because of one mistake, you turn on me!

ED

I'm not turning on you!

TERRY

You are! Accusing me this way!

ED

This is madness! ...

TERRY

Yours then! He broke in here and raped me!

ED

Then why didn't you tell someone then?!

TERRY

Why didn't you?! You knew he had to be killed!

ED

What?! ...

                              TERRY
....Kill him! And go to jail!
                                ED
                    (Crosses to phone)
...I'm calling a doctor.

                              TERRY
                    (Goes to him, stops him)
Why?! Because I'm crazy?! How do you know you're not?! How
do you know there's a blacklist?! There is no fucking blacklist!
You're insane! ...

                                ED
Let go of the phone, dear...

                              TERRY
Let go of the phone, dear....He said you'd turn on me. You have.
Alright, then. Now the truth. He didn't rape me. I gave myself to him!
                                ED
                    (Shaking his head)
Madness! My daughter!
                              TERRY
                    (Shouts raucously)
His power was too much!
His green eyes seduced me!
Ordered me to bed!
Grab me by the head!
Do me till I'm dead!
                    (COOKIE enters as TERRY does an obscene dance
in front of her FATHER)
His eyes the green fires of hell!
                                ED
                          (Grabs her)
Stop it! Stop this!
                            COOKIE
What's going on?

                                ED
She's irrational!

                              TERRY
Let go!
                    (SHE breaks away from him, to ED)
I love him! That's right! He's your tormentor and I love him!

                             COOKIE
                      (Puts down package)
Love who?
                              TERRY
                       (ignores COOKIE)
I know what you Commie bastards are up to!

                             COOKIE
                   (Goes to embrace TERRY)
Terry, what are you saying?

                              TERRY
You're out to destroy this country!
                  (SHE is now backing toward door)
And because I'm for this country, you'll try to kill me!

                             COOKIE
                       (barely audible)
Oh, my God...

                              TERRY
But you don't scare me...
                  (SHE bolts for the front door to escape, but ED
grabs her.)
Let me go!
                                ED
                         (To COOKIE)
Call the doctor.

                               95

TERRY

Let me go! Help! Help! Someone help!

ED

(To the stunned COOKIE again)

Call Josephson!

(COOKIE rushes to telephone and dials.)

TERRY

Please, someone, save me! Murder!

(ED and COOKIE carry her off. The lights change, as Ed comes Back onstage.)

ED

(To audience)

The doctor came, and she was taken away. And the dogs of chaos crouched quietly in the rooms until one day...

LIGHTS: Up on family area.

(ED crosses into it to meet JOE coming out of his room with FRANZ. JOE blocks his FATHER's way)

JOE

(beaming broadly)

Hey, Dad! Where are you going?

ED

To the kitchen.

JOE

No, you're not.

ED

I'm not?

JOE

Golly, Dad, you said not to come back till I could face you directly. Well, I'm back.

ED

To do what?

JOE

Holy cow, Dad, to face you!

ED

(Studies his SON)

Have you been drinking?

JOE

Just a lot, Dad, not a little. Whattaya say, Poppo, let's Indian wrestle!

ED

Oh, Joe, come on...

JOE

A friendly bout. You and I have never played sports together. Except for the footrace through the house when I was a child, which you won. And the wrestle in the upstairs hall, which you also won. But I'm bigger now, and frankly, Father-O, I demand a rematch.

ED

Joe, in the middle of a drizzly afternoon, the last thing I want to do is Indian wrestle.

FRANZ

Afraid, you washed up old lecher?

ED

What? No, I'm not afraid.

FRANZ

The old man says he's not afraid.

JOE

(Slaps FRANZ)

Don't you call my father an old ham. No one can call my father an old ham, 'cause he's not an old ham.

(To ED, gleefully)

JOE(CONT'D)

Whattayasay, Dads, one fall?

(Struck with the inspiration)

And tell you what!

(Holds up FRANZ)

The loser gets him.

ED

What is it, Joe? What's on your mind?

JOE

(throwing his arms wide)

The living room Olympics!

ED

That's all?

JOE

Come on, open up! Trust your fellow man! The people,pops! I'm
one of the people. Trust me!

ED

Alright. Why not?

(Crosses to center of room)

JOE

(Lays FRANZ down on floor betweenthem. Smiling,
extends his hand)

Take my hand.

(THEY grip. Instantly THEY lock in battle at full
strength)

ED

Too hard!

JOE

No! Need it this hard! Force my mouth open! Tell you things!

                              ED

My heart...

                              JOE

I'll kiss it when you're dead...

                              ED

You tricked me!

                              JOE

Facing you...Couldn't before... Too powerful...
        (HE lunges suddenly to throw the FATHER off balance.
              ED instinctively defends and recovers.)
Strong for a sick man.

                              ED

Please, let's stop. Want neither to throw the other!

                              JOE

No. One must be thrown.

                              ED

No! Tell me what's in your heart!

                              JOE

Fury, oh, my king!

                              ED

At what?

                              JOE

At you! At me!

                              ED

Why?

                              JOE

Because I've lied for you! Because I went home the day of that
woman and said nothing!
              (Barely articulate)
Grown up...Grown up...Your fist...In my mouth! Shut me up!

                              ED

I didn't!

                              JOE

Did!

ED

Oh, Joseph, Joe...!

JOE

Dragged me into your battles! Made me march! Damn you, made me take care of weeping wounded!

ED

No one made you!

JOE

Your fist in my soul!

ED

(Coughs)
Alright, I did! Forgive me! Can't you forgive me?!

JOE

Forgive you? Do you forgive the Committee?

ED

They're my enemies! You're not!

JOE

Oh, no? Well, my king, listen to this. For all the times I've dreamed that you and I might play along the beach, for all the times I've yearned to embrace you and feel your father's warmth, for each of those times I've had a time of another kind of vision. In it you were on the beach, alright. But you were on your knees, while I stood over you fully clothed and with a gun at your head, forcing you to commit an act of sexual degradation! My fist in your mouth!

ED

(Thrusts violently against his SON, his fury too strong to be contained.)
You stinking toad...!

JOE

Good! ... Knock me over...I still have that dream!
                    (THEY struggle fiercely, sweating straining, with
only ED's louder wheezing to punctuate the battle.)
You're wheezing, my lord...You cough, my Lord...tell you a
secret...You can't do it...You're muscles old...your days aren't
numbered, oh, my king, they're over! And when you fall...I'll strip
off your robes! Pull you to your knees! ...Put a gun to your head!
And...!

ED

Nehhhh-vehhhr!
                    (In a violent lunge HE raises JOE up high and sends
him crashing to the floor)
No man makes me bow!
                    (Staggers to the window ,out to street.)
You stinking bastards! Murdered my dream! But you can't
murder me!
                    (Waves them up)
Come up here! Come on up! I'll kick your fucking heads in!
                    (Turns around to see JOE on the floor.)
God, what have I done?
                    (Falls to his knees beside the BOY)
Joseph, forgive me!
                    (embraces JOE)
Joe, Joe, I never meant to harm you!

JOE
                    (Gently pushes his FATHER away,reaches for
FRANZ)
I know...I understand...It's alright, Dad...

ED

Please! You are a man! A wonderful, wonderful man!

                    JOE
              (Gets to his feet)
I know...

                    ED
I do love you, son!

                    JOE
I know. Get up, Dad...

                    ED
No! I'm on my knees to you! Here, do what you want!

                    JOE
Dad, please...

                    ED
My son...

LIGHTS:Fade to

              BLACKOUT

              COOKIE'S VOICE
           (In blackout, great alarm)
Ed! Ed! Oh, God, Ed, come here!

              LIGHTS: Up.

                    (ED runs in.)
                    ED
What is it?

                    COOKIE
              (Waving note in air)
He's gone! Joe is gone!

                    ED
What?

                    COOKIE
He's gone!

                      ED
Where? What do you mean?

                    COOKIE
          (Distracted, moving erratically here and there)
Gone! Oh, God, why?
                      ED
          (Takes note from her, reads)
"Dear Mom and Dad, I'm no good anymore, so I'm going away. I
don't know where, but please don't look for me. I love you. I'm
sorry. Joe. "

                    COOKIE
Why?! Why?! We've got to find him! Call the police!

                      ED
          (Knowing why, shaken)
Oh, God, it was me.
                    COOKIE
What? What was you?
                      ED
          (Moves toward phone)
We'll call the police.
                    COOKIE
What was you?
                      ED
          (At phone, dialing)
Nothing.
                    COOKIE
You said something was you! What was it?

                      ED
Cookie, please! I'm trying to call!

COOKIE

No, you said it was you! Did you and Joe fight?

ED

Hello? I'd like the number of the police department...

COOKIE

Did you? Did you yell at him?!

ED

(Trying to listen to phone)

Precinct? No, uh, not any precinct...

COOKIE

What did you do to him?!

ED

Cookie, I can't listen!

COOKIE

What did you do to my son?!

ED

(Torn between her and phone)

I...We...

(Into phone)

What?

(To COOKIE)

No, not a fight, exactly....

(To Phone)

No, uh...My son's missing...

(To COOKIE)

We were Indian wrestling and...

(To phone)

Missing persons?

(To COOKIE)

I threw him, and...

(To phone)

What?

                    COOKIE
                (Deadly quiet)
I want my son.

                                ED
                (Into phone)
Would you repeat that?
                    COOKIE
                (Stronger)
I want my son!
                                ED
Canal 5...
                    COOKIE
Where are my children?! You've driven one mad! The other out of
his home! For what? For your ego? For your child's games?!
                (Indicates his costume)
Look at you! You're a child, but you've robbed me of my children!
Get them back!

                                ED
I can't!

                    COOKIE
You can't! You can't! You can't do anything! You've brought this
down on us! Fix it! Fix it now! Fix it or I'll tear your living heart
out!
                (THEY stare at each other for a moment, then)
Call Kiehl.

                                ED
                (Quietly)
Oh, Cookie, from you?

                    COOKIE
Call him.

ED

Is that what you want, my surrender?

COOKIE

I want my children.
            (He can't speak)
Call him!
            (No words escape him)
Why not? Aren't you man enough?
            (He still can't speak)
You have crimes on your head!

ED

            (Bursts out)
I know that! Am I blind?! Am I deaf?! Every chair, every table
in this place accuses me! You sacrificed your daughter! You
sacrificed your son! Their ghosts are in this room! They walk
into my eyes! They fly into my ears! I hear nothing but innocent
laughter, and then the thought that it was I who stilled it!

COOKIE

And yet you persist! Why? Are you in love with catastrophe?
When will you be satisfied? When I lay gutted on the floor? When
your own mouth is stuffed with ashes? When?

ED

            (Sighs)
I don't know.

COOKIE

            (Goes to him, embraces him)
Stop now. Forget the world, forget the people. They don't care
about us. Let's care about ourselves. Try to reclaim some part of
our lives. It's not too late. The price is small. I'll help you. I'll see
you through it.

                              ED
I can't.

                            COOKIE
Why not?
                              ED
I've given two young lives to the horror. I have to....

                            COOKIE
Even if it kills you?
                              ED
                (calmly, gently, caressing her head)
I'm sorry, sweetheart. I did a cruel thing to you. I carried you so
high, then I brought you down so low.

                            COOKIE
No, no, I love you.
                              ED
    Five years of silence have done their work. I tried to be Balzac
    and nothing happened. I stood here waiting for Madame de
    Berney, but only my children came. That's when I knew. I've
                    become my obsession.
              (COOKIE sits. THEY sit in silence for a long
moment, then)

                            COOKIE
                  (Into her soup, calmly)
I think I have to leave.
                              ED
Yes.
                            COOKIE
I can't go on like this.
                              ED
I know.
                            COOKIE
I'm sorry.

                              107

ED

Please, don't be.

COOKIE
(After another long silence)

It's just that I'm tired.

ED

I understand.
(THEY sit in silence again for a moment)

Where will you go?

COOKIE

To Al. He said I could come.

ED

Good. He'll take care of you.

COOKIE

Yes. And it's a shorter trip to see Terry.

ED

Mm. Not so many subways.

COOKIE
(Another silence, then)

I'm sorry, Ed.

ED
(Reaches across table, takes her hand)

No. You've had enough.

COOKIE
(Matter-of-factly)

I'm tired to the bone.
(Another silence. HE removes his hand)

ED

You go to Al's, let him fatten you up. You're a very pretty woman.

COOKIE

What will you do?

ED

(Shrugs)

What I've been doing. Sit in their offices, walk their streets, stand on their doorsteps. Show up at their restaurants. I'll carry a sign,"Will Act For Food".

COOKIE

(Smiles)

You're still playing a part.

ED

(Smiles)

I know the lines.

(THEY smile at each other. Then COOKIE rises from the table and exits into the shadows.ED, to audience)

That's how we said goodbye. I have a room now in the theater district. I go to see Terry every week. She'll never be well, but she's getting better. I don't see Cookie at all. Joe? ...

(HE gestures into the darkness where his son now resides.)

Sometimes, as I make my way up Broadway, I think and I remember...

At eight o'clock the room was dim,

By nine I spoke with my mother,

At ten I visited with Lear,

And, by eleven, with the brightness, the brightness,

I knew the nature of light.

(HE does a ghostly, faint smile and a flourish)

Para-pati, para-patu.

BLACKOUT

FINAL CURTAIN

MAY DAY

BY
CONRAD BROMBERG

ACT I

SETTING: The stage is in areas. At Left is
                            the house. At Right, the shop.
                            Others are denoted by lighting.

LIGHTS UP ON: The shop. The din of the assembly
                            line moving and of jitneys delivering
                            materials. Overhead the conveyor belt
                            clanks along carrying parts for
                            assembly.

        (GENE, a dark young man with overtly Hebraic
features and a tough New York manner, is moving back and forth
behind the WORKERS on the assembly
line, exhorting as HE goes.)

        GENE
Slow down! Don't go with the line! Gagnon, for Christ sake,
you're running! A normal pace! Tag it, Smitty! Let it go! What is
it, Ortega, you think you're being paid by the car?! You're not!
A normal day's work for a normal day's pay! The contract says
forty cars an hour! This line's going fifty! The company's gets the
profit! You get the heart attack!
        (HE stops)
Is anyone listening?
        (THEY are obviously working too hard to listen to
him. HE takes a step back,
surveys the whole disgusting, inane chaos. HE addresses them in
Yiddish)

113

GENE(CONT'D)

Breder arbeter! Leyght avek ayere makshirim! Tret vikh op fun ayere machinen! Der General Strike iz itzt giltik iber Amerika! In nomen fund dem Dritn Internatzional lad ikh aykh ayn zikh onshlussen in dem ruf far far a baldikn tsuzamentref fun dem Congress fun Communisitishe Delegatn...!

(Through the last part of this HE has been watched by DAVIS, a burly
black man in his mid-thirties, whose laughter can't be heard until the
din of the assembly line, and GENE's speech, are halted by the lunch bell.
Then, in the sudden silence, GENE hears him and turns to him)

DAVIS

What the hell you doing, boy?

GENE

Well, they weren't listening in English, so I threw in a little Yiddish at them.

DAVIS

You threw a lot of Yiddish at 'em. What was all that?
(The TWO MEN cross to meet. DAVIS gives GENE a cigarette and THEY
light up)

GENE

Basically, I invited them to lay down their tools and join the General Strike that would bring Socialism to America.

DAVIS

They must've dug that, all those redneck boys.

GENE

(Points to the now still assembly line)
Hey, did I stop the line or not?

DAVIS

Yes, you did. You and the lunch bell.

GENE

The lunch bell is a major ally of the working class.

DAVIS

But getting written up ain't. And that's what they're gonna give you if they catch you off your station.

GENE

Let 'em write me up. I could use a few days off.

DAVIS

Yeah, but too many write-ups, and you get written out.

GENE

(Sighs, rubs his eyes)

I'm careful.

(Shakes himself to energize himself)

So, what's the poop?

DAVIS

Detroit's coming out for Stevenson.

GENE

Big deal. The lesser evil.

DAVIS

Well, maybe. But I got a feeling for Eisenhower.

GENE

Eisenhower? The man <u>is the Military-Industrial Complex.</u>

DAVIS

That's right. That's why he can end the war in Korea. Stevenson try it, they gonna call him all kinds of a Commie fag, but General Ike do it, and they gonna call him nothin' but SIR.

GENE

Davis, how many times I gotta tell ya? They stop one war, they start another! It's built into the system!

DAVIS

Well, let 'em stop this one, and I'll worry about the next one later.

GENE

Which is just how they want you to play it! One
fucking war at a time!

DAVIS

Gene, I got guys I'm responsible for! Don't throw the party line at
me!

GENE

Why not, if it's right?! You want to stop all wars, change the
fucking game that creates them!

DAVIS

Fine! Next week! So, what you're sayin' is you're for Stevenson?!

GENE

No! He's just Eisenhower in a liberal suit!

DAVIS

Then who? You gonna dig up old Henry Wallace and that
Progressive Party shit again?
            (GENE shrugs reluctantly, suddenly ambivalent)
Then who?

GENE
            (Very quietly)
Bill Foster.

DAVIS

Who?

GENE
            (Louder)
Bill Foster!

DAVIS

Who?!

GENE
(Now combative)
Bill Foster, goddammit! The Party Chairman!

DAVIS
(Half-laughing)
I know he's the Chairman! My question still, Who?! Man, there's
seven thousand cats in this shop. You think any of 'em know who
old Bill Foster is? Three of you young Reds. The three old Reds.
Parker probably knows; me, 'cause I read that shit you give me,
and maybe a couple FBI guys workin' here to keep tabs on you.
For the rest it's Bill who.

GENE
That's not the point.

DAVIS
It is, man. You do better run the Rosenbergs...

GENE
Not funny...

DAVIS
I don't mean it funny. People may hate 'em, but at least they
know who they are. And when they come out for friendship with
Russia, you know they mean it, 'cause their asses may fry for it.
You get all the cuckoo vote and all the spy vote, too.

GENE
I said, not funny! We're running candidates to put out our
independent position on the issues!

DAVIS
To which no one will listen!

GENE
No?! End the war in Korea?! Peaceful coexistence with the Soviet
Union?! End segregating in the South?! You think your own guys
in the Negro Caucus wouldn't listen to that?!

DAVIS

My guys'll listen to anybody! That's the beauty of being on the bottom, man! You' so desperate, you'll listen to anyone who'll listen to you! But they won't vote for you, 'cause it's a throwaway!

GENE

(At the end of his tether)

We don't want their votes! We're just stating our fucking position!

DAVIS

(Suddenly calm, mischievous)

Then why run candidates? It's called an election, so you can vote for one or the other and put-him-in-office.

GENE

(Steps back, scrutinizes DAVIS)

Are you being serious or are you baiting me?

DAVIS

I'm serious. And I'm baiting you.

(THEY BOTH burst out laughing and start to separate)

Hey, Gino.

(GENE stops)

You know that speech? Keep it in Yiddish.

GENE

Of course. You think I want to get killed?

(THEY exit laughing.)

BLACKOUT.

LIGHTS: up on

The house. The living room of a bungalow on the South Side of Los

Angeles. A bunk is at Left near
the Offstage front door. Scattered
around the rest of the wood-wainscotted
room are chairs and sofas and floor
pillows. It is all pick-up furniture,
randomly placed, but the room is neat
and clean. Offstage a radio plays
"Unchained Melody."

(A blond, square-jawed young man, CHAMP, stands in a small cleared
space and does tai Chi Chuan exercises.The doorbell rings, but
HE doesn't stop. From a door leading to hall that runs back the
length of the house, comes GENE.)
                    GENE
He's punctual. He'll learn.
                (HE goes Off to answer the door and returns in a
moment with a third young
man, innocent-seeming, friendly, JOE. HE carries a suitcase.To
Joe.)
We don't hang around the door.
                    JOE
Yeah, I see they're out there. FBI?

                    GENE
Who else? At least we don't have to worry about burglars.
                (HE extends his hand, which JOE takes)
Hi, I'm Gene Glauber.
                    JOE
Joe Morris.
                (CHAMP extends his hand without stopping his
exercise, which JOE
takes with a little difficulty.)
                    GENE
Champ Laughlin. Our club chairman.
                (THEY watch CHAMP move silently)

                    JOE

What is that?

                   CHAMP

Tai Chi Chuan It's real good. You can do it in a prison cell.

                    JOE

Uh-huh. You planning to go to jail?

                   CHAMP

Sooner or later every good communist goes to jail. Ho Chi Minh
did this when the French had him locked up.
                    JOE

Who?

                   GENE

Ho Chi Minh is the Chairman of the Viet Minh.
          (JOE still doesn't know him)
They're fighting the French in Indochina.
                    JOE
              (Nods)
I'm not very political.
          (This stops CHAMP.)
                   CHAMP

Then what are you doing here?
                    JOE

Well, I ran into Hank and told her I needed a job and a place to
stay, and...
          (HE gestures here HE is)

                   CHAMP
              (incredulous)
Did she tell you what we're doing here?

                    JOE

Uh, yeah. You're all from colleges and you're down here working
in factories and leading the workers to Socialism. More or less.

CHAMP

But...you have to be in the Party to do this.

JOE

Oh, yes, I joined. I did everything. Went down to the plant and
applied for the job...and...I start Monday morning.
(The TWO regard him in wonder)

CHAMP

But why?

JOE

Why what?

CHAMP

Well, uh...Do you believe in Socialism?
JOE
(Thinks; then)
Uh, yeah, I guess so.

CHAMP

Do you believe it?! He guesses so!
(In disgust, HE returns to exercising, now working
off his ire in strenuous
push-ups. JOE gives a confused look to GENE)

GENE
(Sotto voce, to JOE)
Don't worry about him. It's just that with all the government
harassment we don't get many people who come here 'cause they
need a cheap place to live.

JOE

Look, I'm willing to do my part...
GENE
Don't worry, you'll do fine. C'mon. I'll give you the tour.
(HE points to the bunk, Left)

GENE(CONT'D)

Put your bags there. That's your bed. The rooms are back there.

(HE points down the hall)

You start out here. When one of us moves out, you get a room, as everyone moves up a room.

(HE starts to lead him out, then stops.)

You do know the Party's illegal.

JOE

Yeah, Hank told me.

GENE

And it doesn't bother you?

JOE

(Thinks, then)

Uh, yeah, a little, I guess...

CHAMP

(in push-ups)

He guesses again! Christ!

(GENE leads JOE down the hall, which can't be seen. Still doing push-ups, muttering to Himself.)

Half the Party leaders are in jail, the other half underground! And he guesses...Oh, man!

(From the back hallway we hear)

GENE (Offstage)

Champ's room in the back...Mine...the John...Kitchen...you can have your own part of the fridge...

JOE (Offstage)

Is this a room? The door's locked.

GENE (Offstage)

Solly's.

(THEY come back into the living room)

JOE

What's that smell?

GENE

Today? Seems like bacon and banana.

JOE

He cooks in there?

GENE

No, he hides food. In his dresser.

JOE

Why?

GENE

He thinks we're stealing from him in the fridge.

JOE

Are you?

GENE

Someone is stealing from all of us. I think it's Solly and he does this to cover. Look, I might as well tell you. We think he's a government informer.

CHAMP

We don't know that.

GENE

There are just too many signs. He's got a super cushy job at the plant. He disappears weekends and other times. He's got a new car and no loan payment book. And more.

JOE

If you think he's a fink, why don't you kick him out?

CHAMP

Then what? They send in a guy we don't know.

GENE

This way he's our fink and we live with him.

CHAMP

Besides, Gene, we can't prove it.

JOE

But doesn't it bother you? This guy selling you out every day?

GENE

What bothers me is he's a Jew. And a putz. And a grabayun!
                (THEY enter the living room again)
So, there you are. Welcome to our house.
                (At this point a stubby, chubby MAN in his early thirties makes himself
known. We don't know how long HE's been there or what HE's heard)

SOL

                (To GENE)
You've been in my room.

GENE

Sol, how could we be in your room? You've got the door locked.

SOL

You'd find a way.

GENE

Sol, I don't need to go in your room to know what's in it. Today's special is bacon and bananas.

SOL

                (To JOE)
What's in my room is my business, don't you agree?

CHAMP

Christ, Sol. What're you worried about?

SOL

Some people don't respect privacy.

GENE

That's great. Privacy between comrades. We're supposed to be ready to lay down our lives for each other, and he wants his privacy.

CHAMP

That's a good point, Sol.Hell, what've we got to hide from each other?

                    (stops exercising)
Who was it who said, "A comrades life should be an open book."

                    SOL

We should all be open books to each other?

                    GENE

Yes.

                    SOL

Share "intimate details?"

                    GENE

Why not? You never know what might affect our work.

                    SOL

Fine. Okay. And to start off, Gene, why don't I drop my pants, and you can smell my asshole?

            (With that HE exits back to his room. The OTHER
THREE stand there, GENE
Flushed with humiliation)

                    GENE

Someday, I'm gonna...
            (to JOE)
See what I mean?

                    JOE

Yeah, I guess.

                    CHAMP

Well, that's Sol, that's all.

                    GENE

No, it isn't all. That's uncomradely behavior. I'm going to bring it up at the next meeting.

CHAMP

You just brought it up.

GENE

But not formally. Not at a meeting.

CHAMP

Gene, any time the four of us get together, it's a meeting. We are the club. And we got important things to do. Not rehash a lot of personal bullshit. We're an advanced unit of the vanguard of the proletariat. Let's act like it.

(HE turns to JOE, puts out his hand)

Welcome to the Frederick Douglass Club of the Labor Youth Organization of the Communist Part of the U.S.A.

(THEY shake hands.)

JOE

(Showing how hip he is)

Frederick Douglas,right! He was this black leader during slavery. Right?!

(He looks around)

Is this supposed to be a Negro club?

GENE

(Stepping in quickly)

We're working on it.

CHAMP

(starts out, stops,jaw tight)

Have you done any reading? Marx? Lenin?

JOE

Eisenstein <u>On Film?</u>

(CHAMP sighs, nods angrily, leaves. JOE takes his suitcase over to his cot.)

GENE

How do you know Hank?

                                    JOE

A girl I know went to school with her. She knew I was pretty
liberal and needed a job and...
                    (HE gestures "that's how it happened."
                    HE sits on the bed to test it)
Where were you before?
                                   GENE

Harvard.
                                    JOE

You have a degree?
                                   GENE

A Master's. Anthropology. I was going for my Ph.D.
                                    JOE

And you quit?
                                   GENE
                    (slightly defensive)
I come from the working class.
                                    JOE

Christ, you could be teaching in college by now.

                                   GENE

        This is where it's happening, brother. With the workers.

                                    JOE

Uh-huh. Where are you from?
                                   GENE

Brooklyn. Brighton Beach. Ever hear of it?
                                    JOE

Yeah. And the others?
                                   GENE

I don't know where Sol is from. He claims he was in the war.
                    (Shrugs skeptically)
He's the kind of Jew I've always hated. Slovenly, rude, full of
gimme and screw you. He's a bad apple.
                                    JOE

And champ?

                                   127

GENE

That's what he is, a champ. A real son of the working class. His dad died organizing the steel union in Youngstown. Champ's a second generation American labor Communist. He's going to be a big leader in the movement, you watch.

JOE

Uh-huh.

GENE

What about you? Where are you from?

JOE

Uh...New York...Well, I grew up in Beverly Hills, but...Well, the poorer part of Beverly Hills. My father was a writer...Not famous. He wrote things like" Tarzan Meets the Nazis"...Like that. When he got blacklisted we moved back to New York...When he died, I moved back here. I thought I'd pick up my old life, but...They had all gone their way and...
(HE trails off, having revealed more than HE wanted to. An awkward silence)

GENE

This a typewriter?
(JOE nods, yes)
You a writer?

JOE

(Shrugs modestly)
I don't know. I write.

GENE

You're not going to have much time for it. We're busy, meetings and such, most nights of the week.

JOE

I'll manage.

GENE

Wait a sec.

GENE(CONT'D)
(GENE leaves into the kitchen. JOE removes the typewriter, looks around
for where to put it, spots the night table by the cot, removes the
lamps to the shelf above and puts the machine on the table. GENE
returns with a gallon bottle and a bucket)

JOE

What's that?

GENE

Brine.

JOE

What for?

GENE

Your hands. Mix this with water, put your hands in, it toughens them.

JOE

For what?

GENE

For work. The metal parts have snags. They'll cut your hands.

JOE

Really? Don't they give you gloves?

GENE

Sure, but you can't wear the gloves and get your operation done
in time. You'll fall behind the line, and they'll fire you. Then
where are we?

JOE

But what about the union? Don't they protect you?

GENE

Not for the first ninety days. That's your probation period. Make
it through that, and you're cool.

JOE

(Getting worried)

How tough is it?

GENE

It's GM, baby. The fastest assembly line in the world. You don't walk on that line, you run. Men have had heart attacks working that line. Men have gone crazy working that line.

(JOE's hand goes to his head)

You run for eight hours a day, and just when you think you've survived it, they announce overtime. We look at overtime the way convicts look at the death penalty.

(JOE starts to sway unsteadily. GENE grabs him)

You okay? What is it?

JOE

No, no, I'm all right. Just sometimes when I get tense, nervous, I go a little fuzzy. I'm fine.

GENE

Don't worry. You'll make it. They give you a couple of weeks to break in, to be behind. After a year or so on the line, you'll have enough seniority to get off it, like the rest of us here. You'll be fine.

BLACKOUT.

Lights up on:

The shop. Day.

(CHAMP enters with DAVIS. THEY watch as the line moves
amid the din of the plant at work. The overhead conveyor carries one raw
metalled car hood after another across the stage)

DAVIS

That your new boy?

CHAMP

Mm.

                    DAVIS
What's his name?

                    CHAMP
Morris. Not too high-level politically, but...These days you take
what you can get.
            (After a moment, a hood with two legs under
    it and two gloved hands gripping it runs back in the other
    directiontoward the assembly line.
    As THEY watch him)

                    DAVIS
Fair move to his left.

                    CHAMP
Not bad. But watch his mount.

                    DAVIS
Ooh. He missed.

                    CHAMP
He's got it caught in the motor.

                    DAVIS
Over the motor, boy! Not in it! The hood goes over the motor!
            (To CHAMP, laughing)
How many cars he behind?

                    CHAMP
Five.

                    DAVIS
Not too bad...

                    CHAMP
For a rookie...

                    DAVIS
Get those gloves off, boy!
            (To CHAMP as JOE runs by them for another hood)
You think he'll make it?

                    CHAMP
            (Shrugs)
I hope. That's a quarter of my club membership right there.

                    131

                    DAVIS
But "One Communist has the strength of ten."
                    (HE winks)
Right?

                    CHAMP
                    (Matter-of-factly)
Right.
                    DAVIS
You really believe that shit?

                    CHAMP
                    (Offended)
Of course I do. Because of our understanding of the dialectical
nature of history. If you understand history, Davis, then you've
got it on your side, and it's a powerhouse ally.
                    DAVIS
Champ, tell me, no shit. Did you ever try to get laid with that line?

                    CHAMP
Well, no.
                    DAVIS
Then don't. You won't make it.
                    (And the hood with two legs and two gloves runs
by, back toward the assembly)
Attaboy, Comrade. Keep humpin'.

                    BLACKOUT

                    LIGHTS: Up on living room. Night.

                    (The ROOMATES sit attentively, except, as always,
for SOL, who lounges by the window,his gaze roaming the street.
The visitor is HENRIETTA WRIGHT ["Hank"]. She is a willowy,
attractive, well-educated young black woman in sweater, with
dickey collar showing above it, and slacks. JOE's hands are sunk
in the brine bucket.)

GENE
(Referring to magazine in front of him)
...So that basically what the Bishop article is saying is that because the Negro people have this four hundred years of oppression under their belt, they are best qualified to judge what is or isn't white chauvinist behavior. Now, granted, this last example is extreme, but I think he chose it on purpose to bring it down to its most personal expression. If a Negro doesn't like to be touched, and a white person touches him, that is a white chauvinist act.

JOE
It doesn't say whether or not the Negro has to tell the white person, "Hey, I don't like to be touched" first. Does he have to?

GENE
Well, why should he? Why should he assume it's an issue, before it's ever happened? That would force the Negro to go around to all the white people he knew and say, "Hey, I don't like to be touched."

JOE
Yeah, but it the white person does it without knowing the Negro doesn't like it, he's getting tagged for white chauvinism for what he thought was an innocent act.

CHAMP
Then let the white person ask the Negro, "Hey do you like to be touched?" Then he'll know in advance.

GENE
Oh, come on. Then you have to go around asking, "Do you like to be touched or looked at or walked behind?" It's crazy.

CHAMP
Well, that's true.
(THEY fall into a puzzled silence. SOL sips the Scotch in his hand)

SOL

What if the Negro wants to be touched, and I don't want to do it?

(HE is looking provocatively at HANK,who blushes,
tenses, as do the OTHERS)

What if a Negro loves me and wants me to touch her, and I don't
love her, so I don't want to? Or pull it to its most extreme. What if
my Negro wants me to rob a bank with her, and I don't want to?
Am I guilty of a racist non-act?

GENE

Your Negro? Do you own Negroes? ...

SOL

Excuse me, my symbolic Negro...

GENE

...I don't like your tone...!

SOL

...You don't like my question...

CHAMP

All right, all right, calm down... Hank?

HANK

(Thinks, then)

Well, as one of "your Negroes," I think the "touching" example is
unfortunate. I think the intent of the article is to move Negroes
to take responsibility for defining and speaking out about acts
taken against them. Not to rely on their white friends, as they
have traditionally. And, yes, Sol, I felt a...an innuendo in your
voice.

CHAMP

Yeah. A sexual one...

GENE

And a racial one...

SOL

(Thinks, then)

I accept. Let me examine myself self-critically.

(Wherein HE studies his crotch with great critical
eye. Joe Bursts out
laughing. The OTHERS don't.)

BLACKOUT.

LIGHTS:Up on The Shop. The water cooler.

(CHAMP and DAVIS pour cups and drink)

                    DAVIS
How's your boy doing?
                    CHAMP
Toughening up.
                    DAVIS
He off the gloves?
                    CHAMP
Just about.
                    DAVIS
Good.
          (THEY drink)
I read that Bishop article.
          (CHAMP sighs visibly. DAVIS jumps back in mock
horror.)
Don't touch me!
          (HE cracks himself up, as CHAMP gestures
helplessly.)
Do you believe that shit?!
          (HE subsides.)
Hey, you gonna grow hair on your palms from reading that stuff.
Who gives a shit about all that "touchin'"? I got real problems
here. Gettin' more black men in the door here! Gettin' 'em
through the probation period safe! Gettin' 'em assigned to other
than the motherfuckin' paint shop, which we all know is Death
Valley! Man, tell that to this Bishop chump!

CHAMP

Well, that's why we're on the Fair Practices Committee.

DAVIS

That's fine, and I appreciate it, but I need some white boys on that committee.

CHAMP

What're you talking about? We're white.

DAVIS

No, Champ, you're Red. And everybody knows it. You get me one real, down home, red-neck, peckerwood white boy to stand up at the union meeting and say, "We better get with the niggers here or we ain't gonna get with nothing.: You get me a white boy like that, and I'll let you touch me anywhere you want.

BLACKOUT.

LIGHTS:Up on

"Red Square," our boys' shop hangout.
An island of shipping pallets on the
Assembly line of the auto factory.
Sun filters in through the grimy
Windows. The small area has been made
Into a resting spot by lining the wooden
Pallets with newspapers, an old slashed
Auto seat and some packing material.

(JOE sits next to a young worker named KELLER who is perusing the daily Qracing page of the paper, while eating. JOE Doesn't eat, but ostentatiously "reads"His paper, a left-wing monthly whose headline proclaims, "Chinese Youth In Bowling Leagues." JOE shakes his head in awe of what HE is "reading," makes Loud sounds of surprise and admiration.Finally, KELLER turns to see what it's about, as an Offstage radio plays "ComeOn 'A My House" with Nellie Lutcher.)

                              JOE
Incredible.
                             KELLER
What?
                              JOE
This.
                             KELLER
What?
                              JOE
                            (Reads)
..."Over 18 million Chinese youth participate on a regular basis in
a local or regional bowling league."
                    (HE turns to KELLER as if to say, "isn't that
something?"
                    (Keller feels HE is being addressed from Mars.)
You bowl?
                             KELLER
                            (Shrugs)
Sometimes.

                              JOE
                         (Triumphantly)
Well, there you go.
                             KELLER
There I go what?
                              JOE
                      (Trying to make it reach)
Well, you know...You bowl, they bowl...
                    (HE makes gestures trying to indicate that
KELLER, HE, and the Chinese youth are brothers in bowling.
KELLER watches, stupefied but fascinated by
this weird performance)
Well, I mean, you know how they're always depicting the Chinese
as slant-eyed, yellow hordes and shit like that. Not as, you know,
normal people like us...But here...
                    (HE indicates paper)

JOE(CONT'D)

...You can see. Eighteen million kids going down to the lanes every Thursday...Just like us.

KELLER

Uh-huh. Tell me, do they bowl like this? ...

(HE draws an imaginary verticle line.)

Or like this?

(HE flashes a smile full of jagged, rotting teeth,draws a horizontal line.)

JOE

(Sad smile)

Yeah...Well...

KELLER

You know, I thought about that. That whole thing of Chinks having sideways pussies? It's not humanly possible. 'Cause they's only maybe three inches across down there. You could maybe get your dick in but you could never get the baby out. And them Chinks drop litters like flies. So I know they don't have no sideways pussies...

JOE

(weakly)

Well, you see...Just like us.

KELLER

(Conjectures)

...Unless, of course, they's babies come out sort of in the shape of a hot dog...

JOE

...I doubt that...

KELLER

...In which case it would be possible...

JOE

Well, if that was so, yes, but...I don't think babies anywhere come out like...in that shape...

KELLER

I dunno. You ever seen a Chinese whelp? I mean newborn? ...

JOE

Well, no, but...

KELLER

Well, then, ya see? You don't know. Do ya?

JOE

Well, not from personal observation, no, but...Medical science
tells us...

KELLER

Tells us? Shit, boy.
        (HE points to the assembly line.)
The company <u>tells us</u> this line's doin' forty cars an hour, but I <u>see</u>
it doin' fifty-four...

JOE

That's true, right. What do you think about it?

KELLER

I don't think shit about it.
        (Eyes JOE evilly.)
I'll tell you what else I mean. A Chink with a dick growing out of
his mouth.
        (JOE sighs, sees his efforts going aglimmering.)
You don't believe me? Here.
        (HE pulls out his wallet, fishes a photo from it,
hands it to JOE,who looks, winces.)

JOE

Is that in Korea?
HE points to someone in the photo.)
Is that you?

KELLER

Two years ago.

        (HE takes the picture back, rises.)

What's your name, boy?

JOE

Joe.

KELLER

Joe what?

JOE

Morris.

KELLER

Your daddy change it from Morris-stein?

JOE

        (Struck)

No.

KELLER

But you're Jewish.

        (JOE says nothing.)

What the hell you doin' here?

JOE

I need a job.

KELLER

        (Guffaws)

And I need a case of crabs! Why ain't you working in your daddy's store?

JOE

He doesn't have a store ...

KELLER

C'mon. Your people don't take care of you? Shit. Jews always take care of they own...

JOE

        (Shrugs apologetically.)

What can I tell ya?

        (KELLER studies him for a long moment.)

KELLER

What are you doin' here?

JOE

Workin'. Just like you.

KELLER

(Skeptical, thinks)

I killed that feller in the picture.

JOE

Okay. How do you feel about it?

KELLER

Why? Is he your brother?

JOE

(Weaseling with dignity.)

Well, maybe...metaphorically...

KELLER

Meta-whatically?

JOE

It's a term...

KELLER

If he is, you take care.

(HE leaves. JOE sinks back against the pallet, relieved, guilty.)

BLACKOUT.

LIGHTS: up on

The Living room of the house. Early
Evening.

(The FOUR ROOMATES sit around, except SOL who leans near
the window, half looking out, drink in hand.)

CHAMP

...So what we're looking for is one white worker, not associated with us; in fact, he can pretend not even to know us, to go on Davis's Fair Practices Committee.

141

GENE

And if he's from Mississippi so much the better.

CHAMP

Not easy, I know. But if we find him, we score heavy with Davis.
            (This is received with skeptical sounds by GENE
and JOE)
            Okay. <u>Red Flag</u> subscription drive. To lead it off. I
talked to... (HE consults his pocket notebook.)
Seven white workers, four Mexican, and four Negro since last
week. Of those, I sold one sub to a Negro worker and I've got two
white and one Mexican worker interested. Since the drive started
that brings me up to twelve subscriptions.
            (HE turns to GENE, who consults his little
notebook.)

GENE

That's great, twelve. Okay, talked to three white, two Negro,
four Mexican. I have two Negroes definitely interested and I'm
nearing a sale to one of last week's Mexicans. So, for the drive,
I'm at seven subs.

CHAMP

Good. Keep at 'em. Sol?
                SOL
            (Turns from window)
Ah...Well...I talked to a few people...A couple look good...I'll know
more next week.

CHAMP

So, how many subscriptions have you sold, all told?

SOL

So far? Uh...let's see...
                CHAMP

None.

SOL

None. I guess that's right.

CHAMP

I guess that's right. What if Lenin had been asked how many subs he had sold, and he hadn't sold any? Would he have just shrugged and said, "I guess that's right"?

GENE

First of all, Lenin wouldn't be caught dead not having sold a sub...

CHAMP

But if he hadn't sold any? What would his attitude be?

SOL

(Thinks)

Well...Let's see...Lenin in Russia or Lenin in Switzerland?

GENE

What the hell has that got to do with it?

SOL

Well, it'd probably be tougher to sell in Switzerland. All those people skiing or running hotels.

GENE

Oh, man, be serious!

SOL

I am. There aren't that many workers in Switzerland.

GENE

Self-critical! Lenin would be self-critical! He'd be all over himself with, "What am I doing wrong?! Is my approach right?! Am I talking to the right workers?!"

SOL

Well, yes, I guess he would be, if he was in Russia...

GENE

No matter where he was, you idiot!

CHAMP

All right. The point is, Sol, if you're not doing well with something, you shouldn't leave it to your comrades to bring it up, you should be questioning yourself about it.
            (SOL just looks at him.)
Right?
                        SOL

Okay.

CHAMP
            (Sighs)
All right. Now, Joe. I know you're new to all this, so we don't expect too much from you right away. So, if you have nothing to report...

JOE
            (Soaking his hands in the brine tub)
Yeah, well, I'm still trying to keep up with the line. And I try to recuperate at lunch...

GENE

We understand...
                        JOE

...But I did talk to one Mexican worker and one white worker. The Mexican worker didn't read English...
                        CHAMP

We've got to come out with a Spanish language edition...!

JOE

...But the white worker listened...And we discussed it...

GENE

Good, good...

JOE

...And it led us into a discussion of the Korea war...

CHAMP

Great! ...

JOE

Maybe yes, maybe no. The way we left it was that he was going to think over whether or not he was going to kill me and stuff my balls in my mouth.
                (This deflates GENE and CHAMP.)

GENE

Oh. Yeah, one of them. A real faputzit goy, huh?

JOE

But I'll keep trying. I mean, talking to the workers and all.

CHAMP

Yeah. Good.
                (HE consults the agenda)
Okay. That's it. Good meeting.

GENE

Wait. Ho. What about May Day?

CHAMP

What about it?

GENE

What are we going to do this year? I thought last year was good, that mass meeting downtown at the Ballroom.

CHAMP

Yeah, well...I think they have something special in mind for this year.

GENE

Really? What? Can you tell?

CHAMP

I don't know. Hank just said, something special. It's coming down from National.

GENE

National?! Wow!
(to JOE)
National is the National Committee of the Party! New York! Wow!
That's exciting!

SOL

Are we adjourned?

CHAMP

Adjourned.
(SOL leads the way back through the door to the
bedrooms, followed by
CHAMP. JOE stops GENE, pulls him back into the room.)

JOE

Listen, I'm sorry to put a damper on the <u>Red Flag</u>
discussion, but...I don't know how you've sold seven subs. I
mean, this one guy I talked to was absolutely virulent. And from
the talk I've heard in the shop...I don't know how you do it. (Now
GENE takes JOE aside.)

GENE

(In a low tone)
Don't worry about it. Look, really try to sell them, okay? But if
you can't, here's what you do: The guys you talk to, somehow find
out their full name. You make out the subscription slip in their
name, care of your name at this address. And you give it in to
Champ with the money to pay for it.

JOE

And then what happens when the papers come here?

GENE

As far as Sol, the prick, is concerned, we take 'em into the shop
and give 'em to the guys who subscribed.

                             JOE

And do you?

                             GENE

Are you kidding? I like my balls where they are.

                             JOE

So, what do you do?

                             GENE

We wait till Sol, that fat fuck, is out of the house and...We burn them.
                             JOE

Champ does it too?

                             GENE

Everyone does it. Guys in all the shops.
                             JOE

Excuse me, but...isn't that sort of deceiving the leadership?

                             GENE

Does the leadership want the truth? We tried at first. The paper
almost went under. There was a lot of self-criticism. Some people
were replaced. We learned our lesson. Now everybody's happy.

                          BLACKOUT.

                        LIGHTS: up on

The living room of the house. Night.

                 (The visitor is again HANK)

                            CHAMP

...So to wrap up, the GM club has a total of 28 subs for the drive.
                 (HE hands the stack of subscription forms across
the table to HANK)
And 280 bucks...
                 (HE hands her cash in an envelope)
And we end up seven subs over our quota.

ALL

Yea. Hot dog. Great.

HANK

(Flushed with good feeling)

I certainly do accept this on behalf of Division. And I congratulate you all. Really, comrades, excellent work.

(The COMRADES are properly modest)

You by far surpassed all the other industrial clubs.

(Our SURPASSERS are cool)

And a special nod to our new member...

(SHE turns to JOE)

...Who, in a very short time, sold six subscriptions.

(The OTHERS applaud JOE, who blushes with shame that passes for modesty)

Now... I want to read you a letter. From the National Committee.

HANK(CON'D)

(The BOYS thrill. SHE reads. SOL drinks.)

"To the Industrial Youth Clubs. Greetings. Over the past few years our Party has been on the defensive. We've conducted an exhausting battle in the courts to defend our rights under the Constitution. We will win that fight. Already there are signs the tide is turning. Most notably the standstill in the war in Korea. The forces of Kim Il Sung, along with their Chinese allies, have practically driven the puppet Synghman Rhee's troops and the American forces that prop up his regime out of North Korea. In light of this, the National Committee of the Party has decided it's time for us to counterattack. To press our demands for an immediate cease fire in Korea and the immediate withdrawal of American troops. To this end we propose a march and a rally on May Day. In many cities throughout the nation these marches will be held. Let us say with a loud and public voice that we join hands for peace with our Soviet brothers and sisters!

(The GUYS applaud lustily.)

GENE

Great! Fantastic! A huge march!

CHAMP

Oh, man, thousands!

JOE

Yeah! Where's it going to be?!

HANK

In your shop.
(The GUYS stop dead)

GENE

Beg pardon?

HANK

The youth are going to lead the marches on campuses and in factories. In shops like yours, where you have so successfully rallied the young workers to an acceptance in the sub drive, that's where we want to stage our march!
(A vast silence overcomes our RALLIERS OF THE WORKERS.)

GENE

Well. It's a great idea. Just what...did you have in mind?

HANK

Haven't you always dreamed of marching up the main aisle of GM holding aloft the banners of the American flag side by side with that of the Soviet Union? This is the time!

JOE

Jesus...

GENE

Right up the center aisle? ... Well, yes. But....you know there are very strong right-wing forces in the shop.

JOE

Yeah, strong...

                    HANK

True. But are they going to risk alienating the young workers
who now accept you by trying something funny? Especially if
some of those young people join you in the march, which we
hope and believe they will. We'll put out leaflets well in advance.
You can have meetings leading up to it to discuss the issues with
them. By the day of the march you could have hundreds with you.
What are Parker and his goons going to do in the face of that?

                    SOL

Kill us.

                    HANK

Guys, listen to me. You've built a mass base in that shop.
            (SHE holds up the subscription blanks)
These prove it. These people may not agree with you. But they
respect you, listen to you. Comrades, we're ready!

                    CHAMP

Yes. We can do it. We can.

                    SOL

It's crazy. It's suicide.

                    CHAMP

It's a moment in history.

                    GENE
            (Having studied them)
Yes, I agree. We can do it. It'll be tough, but...
            (JOE is about to say something)
Don't worry about it. I call for the vote.

                    SOL

I call for discussion.

                    GENE

We just did that.

                    SOL

Four of us marching down a thousand feet of gauntlet, holding
high the American and Soviet flags? That is the kamikaze move of
all time!

                          GENE
Okay? Said your piece?

                         CHAMP
It's the juncture of the workers and history. When my old man
and his comrades walked into Youngstown Steel that morning
in '37, they were told the same thing. These boys aren't ready.
They'll beat you up and throw the union out! But the comrades
didn't listen! They knew! And my old man said it! "This is the day
the men of Youngstown Steel sit down and take this plant!" And
goddammit, they did! Call the question!

                          GENE
Aye!

                         CHAMP
Aye!

                           JOE
                     (Uneasy)
Aye.

                          SOL
                 (Grunts a laugh)
You're all crazy.

                         CHAMP
Passed! Unanimously! Meeting adjourned!
                (HANK rises and applauds each of our heroes in
turn. THEY join her, until ALL, except SOL, are
                    CHAMP (CONT'D)
                applauding. It dies down. SOL folds up on The
couch to read a magazine. CHAMP goes to HANK.)

                         CHAMP
Could I see you for a minute, Comrade?
                (SHE nods as discretely as possible and THEY exit
to the back hall.)
I wanted to get your thinking on the shop elections coming up...
                (And THEY are gone. JOE pulls GENE into his part
of the living room.)

                          151

JOE
(Sotto voce)
Don't worry about it? They're going to get us killed!

GENE
I said don't worry. It's never going to happen.

JOE
We just voted on it!

GENE
Let me ask you something. How man Soviet flags do you think
there are in the Greater Los Angeles area? Let's say twenty. But
you know the other clubs are gonna grab them up. If I volunteer
to get the flags and take my time about it, there won't be any
Soviet Flags left. Anywhere. No red flag, no march.

JOE
We could make one.
GENE
Not if I come up empty the night before the march.

JOE
Yeah. But then what will we do instead. We have to do something.

GENE
Like normal, sane people, we'll hand out leaflets.

JOE
You think that's enough? You think Champ'll go for it? I mean, it's
not very...

GENE
...Brave? Dramatic? Who says brave is always best? We're all so
worried about our courage...

                    JOE

I'm not! ...

                    GENE

Of course you are!

                    JOE

No, listen, really...!

                    GENE

No, I understand!

                    JOE

You don't! People always get the wrong idea. It has nothing to do
with courage. It has to do with my childhood. A question came
up. One morning when I was eight years old and staying home
form school. I was playing on the stairs. I suddenly look up and
there above me is this giant in a white robe, my father, just woken
up at noon. He looks down at me and says, "What the hell are you
doing here?!" It was the first time I experienced the dizziness
you know about. Did he mean simply, "Why are you home from
school this morning?" Or was it deeper? "What are you doing
here?" meaning, "What are you doing on this earth, what is your
purpose?" A tough one for an eight-year-old. But then, maybe it
was the big one, "What the <u>hell</u> are you doing here?!" Implying
maybe I shouldn't be here at all, no matter what my purpose.
Whatever he meant by it then, that question is with me to this
day. You guys have strong convictions to help you face whatever
armed struggle. I'm not that advanced.

                    GENE

I understand.

                    JOE

I'll help the club however I can...

                    GENE

I know...

                    JOE

But the thought of marching down that aisle...

                              GENE

It won't happen...

                              JOE

I believe in Socialism. I believe in the Revolution. I just hope, pray
we can vote it in.

                              GENE

I agree with you a hundred per cent. Communists are not violent
people.

                              JOE

Right. Okay. I feel better. And this is just between us.

                              GENE
                    (Locks his lips)
Sealed.
                    (A female sound is heard from CHAMP's room at
the back of the house. The
THREE MEN in front hear it. Another female sound. GENE turns
away)

                              JOE

What the hell is that?
                              GENE
It's all right. They're going to get married.
                              SOL
Mmm. Sounds like she's giving him leadership.
                    (Now a male sound responds.)
Now he's giving leadership.
                    (Now male and female voices intermingle.)
They're giving each other leadership.
                    (The voices rise together in a crescendo of sound.)
My god, are they giving leadership!
                    (JOE suppresses a giggle, but GENE turns savagely
on SOL.)

GENE

Shut up.

SOL

(Innocently)

I was just commenting ...

GENE

You and your wise mouth! They love each other!

SOL

Well, let 'em do it somewhere else. They're keeping me from my room.

(The sounds now reach climax. It clearly strikes GENE to the heart.)

GENE

That's the sound of the future, for your information! Golden children will come from that! So, if you don't like it, it's too goddamn bad!

SOL

(Studies GENE)

Well, well, Gino, old dear. Do I detect a bit of jealousy in your voice? A little hankering after our beloved lady leader?

(GENE turns away)

Oh, my! We do want a little taste of black leadership, don't we?

(GENE rushes over, grabs SOL by the shirt.)

GENE

Get up! Get up! I'm gonna kick your fucking racist ass in!

(SOL instantly goes limp, smiles)

SOL

You are attacking a follower of Mahatma Gandhi.

GENE

Get up! Get up!

(And the THREE MEN listen again to a second climax from the back room.)

BLACKOUT.

LIGHTS UP ON:

"Red Square." Lunch time.

     (And for a second time, JOE finds himself alone, eating with KELLER. This time JOE doesn't pretend to read <u>Red Flag</u>. HE eats and reads a novel. KELLER
Eats and casts periodic glances at him, as the Offstage radio plays"Ghost Riders In The Sky" with Vaughn Monroe.)

             KELLER

Give up your paper route?

             JOE

What?

             KELLER

<u>Red Flag</u>.

             JOE

Oh. Well, no...I can get you one if you want.

KELLER No thanks.
        (THEY lapse into silence)
Are you guys really gonna bring a Russian flag in here?

             JOE
        (Looks up)
Why not?

             KELLER

And march it up the aisle there?
             JOE
        (Trying for calm and courage)
That's the plan.

KELLER
(Shakes his head in wonder)
Did Moscow tell you to do it? Or are you insane enough to think it up yourselves.

JOE
(Sighs with anxiety)
No, it's our idea.

KELLER
In-sane.
(Another silence)
You realize what Parker's boys gonna do, eat you up. Have you seen what they got? Those slats they cut into clubs? Some with nails through 'em? They're gonna bash your brains, boy, all over the floor!
(JOE's hand goes to his head)
You hear me.

JOE
(Feebly)
We have the right to march.

KELLER
You got the right to die!
JOE
(Despite himself, explodes)
Well, what the hell is it to you?! If I want to die, it's my business! Nothing to do with you!

KELLER
Damn right!
(Another silence, where JOE collects himself.)

JOE
(Quietly)
I didn't mean you. Sorry.

KELLER

(Shrugs)

Yell all you want. Fuck don't bother me.

JOE

No, I don't believe in it. You don't get anywhere yelling.

KELLER

You realize you are from Mars, don't you?

(JOE beholds him from Mars.)

I mean, just out of curiosity, do you believe in Communism enough to die for it?

(JOE has no answer, thinks, then)

JOE

You went to Korea. Did you believe in that?

KELLER

Hey, boy, I got drafted.

JOE

So did I.

KELLER

And you're ready to die for it, just 'cause someone told you to?

JOE

Yeah, just like you.

(And this gives KELLER pause.)

KELLER

Well, what the hell do you believe in?

JOE

"What the hell are you doing here?"

KELLER

What?

JOE

Nothing.
(Thinks)
I don't know what I believe in. Do you?

KELLER

Hell, yes. A '52 Merc V8, cut down, four-barrel, customized, shootin' down the highway at 100 per with the best piece of Southgate pussy in one hand and a bottle of Jack D in the other.

JOE

Well, I don't know how that stacks up against world socialism, but...

KELLER

It got me through Korea. What's gonna get you through that march? Lox and bagels and the Sunday New York Times?
(JOE looks at him. How does this red-neck know about that?)
Well, just 'cause I'm dumb don't make me stupid. The Three Families used to have lox and bagels flown in from Cincinnati. I delivered it to they houses. Along with the Sunday New York Times. They offered me that lox fish, and I tried it, but I didn't much like it. It sort of tastes like when you go down on a girl. But if that's what they like, and it reminds 'em of that, well, more power to 'em. And they'd sit there and read what all over the world was doin', so they'd know what to do in Olaka in business the next week. See? I know my Jews. They never do nothin' ain't got some purpose. Even eatin' that pussy-fish and readin' that paper. They was keepin' in touch with The World Organization.

JOE

(Appalled)
Do you really believe that?

KELLER

Do you really not?

JOE

No!

KELLER

No? Do you like lox and bagels?

JOE

Well, yes, but...

KELLER

And the Sunday <u>Times</u>?

JOE

...Sometimes, but...

KELLER

Well, there you go.
            (JOE sighs, shakes his head in defeated disbelief.)
'Course, how you get from there to Communism, I don't know.

JOE

It's the bad side of the family. We read books, throw bombs...

KELLER

... And march for Russia.

JOE

            (Another sigh to repress his frustration.)
Do you really think that's why we're marching?

KELLER

Well, ain't it?

JOE

            (Jumps up, losing control.)
Peace! Peace! The fucking brotherhood of man, you shmuck! So
numb-nuts like you don't have to go to war! ... And...
            (HE gropes for words.)
Love! ... Love! It's all about love and...brotherhood! And...ALL
loving each other! And...Living together in peace! And...

KELLER

...Right. The Russkies taking over...

        (JOE stops, sees himself flailing his arms helplessly, controls himself.
HE very calmly resumes his seat, picks up his book, and reads.
But HE can't.)

JOE

Look. Answer me something. Do you really want on your gravestone, "He died for a car, a bottle and a piece of ass"? Is that really all you want? I mean, you're a human being. You live on this earth. You must have thoughts and dreams and....

KELLER

      (Thinks, then)

Yes...I do.

JOE

Some thoughts of how to live with your fellow man...Some dream of a better way, a deeper goal.

KELLER

I do.

JOE

What? Tell me.

KELLER

I'd like to own an apartment house in Redondo Beach.

      (JOE digests this, looks the OTHER in the eye)

JOE

Well...if that's the case...In all humility I think you ought to re-examine your whole life. Now, if you'll excuse me, I'm going to read my book by Thomas Mann, a famous Martian writer, which traces the rise of Naziism using the Faustian metaphor.

      (JOE ostentatiously reads. KELLER is stung by this rebuke to his ignorance, hides it. After a moment, HE rises, looks around casually.)

JOE(CONT'D)

KELLER

Well, that's fine. As long as you're ready to die for it.
(HE saunters off. JOE drops the book, sighs.)

JOE
(To the stacks)
What the hell am I doing here?

BLACKOUT

END OF ACT I

ACT II

SCENE: The house. Late Sunday afternoon.
          The Sunday L.A. papers are strewn
          over the living room floor and
          furniture.

(HANK, clad in halter and shorts,enters carrying a cup of coffee.)

HANK

Darling, you can't have Negro Nationalism when you have Socialism.
(SHE puts down coffee and begins topick up papers.)
Black bourgeoise nationalism is a capitalist phase of development.
(CHAMP, dressed in jeans and unbuttoned,loose, short-sleeve sport shirt, enters with a cup of coffee.)

CHAMP

But you can't just skip that phase.
(HE joins her in collecting papers, neatening the room,.)

HANK

It's been skipped for us. When we get Socialism here, we're going to declare the Negro Nation. The Socialist Negro Nation. Alabama, Arkansas, Mississippi, all those states with all their industries will be ours. If we all own Bessemer Steel, why would one of us want to start a private steel company? We're going to have it all.
(SHE stops her labors, struck by an idea.)
My god! Can you imagine the first black-produced automobile?! We'll call it...The Sojourner, after Sojourner Truth!
(Inventing as SHE goes)

163

HANK(CONT'D)

We'll name everything after our heroes! ...The Frederick
Douglass National Bank! The, uh...Denmark Vesey Power and
Light! ...
                    (CHAMP has stopped picking up, watches her with
quiet affection.)
Robeson Studios Presents! ... And in radio and TV, in honor of Nat
Turner...Turner Broadcasting!
                    (SHE ends up right in front of him. HE puts his
arms around her waist,
SHE around his neck. SHE softens in his arms)
Don't you see it? Isn't it wondrous?

                         CHAMP

I hope you get it.

                         HANK

You'll be there. "Champ Laughlin, First Secretary, Communist
Workers Party, U.S.A"
                    (HE smiles wistfully, already seeing his fate)
What is it? Hon?
                    (HE slowly disengages himself from her, pulls an
envelope from his back
pocket, hands it to her.)
What's this?

                         CHAMP

The pink slip to my car.

                         HANK

What? ... Why?

                         CHAMP

Just in case.

                         HANK
In case of what?

                         CHAMP
                 (Shrugs, trying to make little of it)
Something happens to me.

                         HANK
                 (Doesn't get it. Then SHE does)
What? ... You mean on the march? But why? You've got all that
support.

                         CHAMP

Because I'm the leader.

                         HANK

But you've got all that support.

                         CHAMP
So did my dad back in '37, but the company goons came after
him.
                 (Alarmed, SHE rushes into his arms.)

                         HANK
Oh, honey, no! Don't even think that way!

                         CHAMP
                 (Pats her reassuringly)
No, no, I'll be fine. It's just...You have to be ready...

                         HANK
Oh, Champ! ... Champ!

                    BLACKOUT.

                    LIGHTS: up onthe house. Late afternoon,
                    two days Later.

                         165

(JOE, still in work clothes, sits on his bed, staring in disbelief at a flyer in his hand.)

JOE

Irving Feibel?

GENE (Offstage)
I just want to thank you for breaking my heart! Jesus Christ! Two years we've been together, and you never told me!
CHAMP (Offstage)
You know it's a Feebee frame job!
GENE (Offstage)
Sure it is! But it's you!
(CHAMP enters with GENE in hot pursuit)
All those stories! Youngstown! Your father! The great sitdown strike of '37! Lies!

JOE

(To CHAMP)
Your name is Irving Feibel?

GENE

Our working-class hero is a fraud!

JOE

That's your real name?

GENE

Not only that, but we've got to hear it from Parker!
(Grabs JOE's flyer, holds it to CHAMP's face.)
Replete with high-school pictures from Edison, New Jersey!
(Now CHAMP turns on him.)

CHAMP

Did you get the flag, Gene?!

GENE

No, Irving, I didn't get the flag! Why get the flag just to be laughed at as we march along?! Laughed at! Just like today! And tomorrow and the next day! Our real American is just another Jew-boy! The Four Jews-keteers! That's all we are now!

CHAMP

You've had six weeks to get that goddamn flag! Why haven't you got it?!

GENE

I haven't got an Israeli flag either! 'Cause that's what we should march under! The Semites Club of the Labor Youth Organization! Damn it, Champ or Irving, or whatever the hell your real name is, how could you do this to me? To us?!

CHAMP

Champ Laughlin is my name! I changed it legally when I was eighteen! I have nothing in common with Irving Feibel! I never did!

GENE

It's your heritage, for Christ sake!

CHAMP

Heritage?! What, my old man with his hole-in-the-wall clothing store?! His loftiest goal was to buy up remnants at thirty percent and sell at sixty! My mother?! To beat Ida Felspar at canasta!

GENE

It's who you are!

CHAMP

No! It's nothingness! I grew up with two dead people in a town of dead people! I walked out of these and became myself!

167

GENE

Yourself! A self that lies to his comrades?!

CHAMP

To inspire you! To give you the strength that I felt! Whether he had any sons or not, I am the natural heir of Daniel Laughlin who died in the mill at Youngstown Steel!

        (SOL appears in the hallway door,leaning against it, watching.)

Why are you so shocked, for god sake? Who is Vladimir Ulianov? He is Lenin! Lenin the Lion! Joseph Djugashvili? Stalin, the man of steel! Are the workers going to rally behind Irving Feibel?!

SOL

No, but the accountants might.

CHAMP

        (Ignoring him)

Champ Laughlin is who I am. The rest I left behind me.

GENE

Until today.

CHAMP

It'll blow over.

GENE

You think so? With Parker there to remind them of it? You have dealt this club a blow.

SOL

        (Sings lightly)

"Just another Jew,
Everything I goo..."

        (The anger washes out of GENE. HE collapses on the sofa.)

GENE

Oh, shit. It's all over.

>   (A pause in which CHAMP gathers himself to take
> the offensive.)

CHAMP

>   (To GENE)

Why didn't you get us a Soviet flag?

GENE

I tried. There weren't any. The other clubs must have scooped
them up early.

JOE

>   (Mr. Reason)

Well, without a Soviet flag to go with the American flag, I don't
think it would make much sense to march.

SOL

How about a sign that says, "Soviet Flag"?

>   (HE doesn't get a laugh.)

SOL

Does Hank know about this? Her all-American boy is just another
Yidloch?

CHAMP

You stay out of this.

SOL

She doesn't.

JOE

Maybe we could make up a couple of signs that say, "Peace," and
have the rally at the relief station and give out leaflets.

SOL

The name of the painting is "Four Yids With Leaflets." It's universal, seen around the world.

CHAMP

(To GENE)

Goddamnit, why didn't you get the flag?!

(SOL disappears into his room.)

You had six fucking weeks to get it! I ask one simple thing of you!

...

GENE

There weren't any, Irving! I went everywhere!

JOE

There couldn't have been too many around. What with the anti-Soviet hysteria and all, people probably burned theirs.

GENE

Absolutely. Gone. None left.

(SOL re-enters, drops a packet on the coffee table.)

CHAMP

What's that?

SOL

Open it.

(Cautiously, CHAMP removes the brown paper to reveal a folded red cloth.

HE slowly unfolds it, revealing a four-by-seven-foot Soviet flag.

JOE faints. SOL disappears into the kitchen.)

GENE (Rushes to Joe)

Joe, what is it?! What happened?!

CHAMP

He fainted!

GENE

Knees up! Put a pillow under his head! Let the blood run out!

CHAMP

No, the head down! Let the blood come back!

GENE

No, too much blood to the brain!

CHAMP

No, idiot, not enough!

GENE

Says who?! Did you take Life-Saving class...?!
                (SOL comes in with a glass of water, as JOE comes
to.)
Don't move! You're all right!

CHAMP

What happened? You just keeled over.
                (SOL hands the water to JOE, who sips it.)

SOL

The thrill of marching got to him.

CHAMP

You're okay. Take it easy.
                (It quiets down, as JOE recovers in a watchful
silence.)

JOE

I'm okay. This happens. Sorry.

> (The OTHERS gradually drift back to the flag.)

CHAMP

> (Admiring it)

We march.

GENE

> (To SOL, accusingly)

Where did you get this?

SOL

What do you care?

GENE

> (To CHAMP)

There isn't a Soviet flag in the entire metropolitan area, and he comes up with one! How?!

CHAMP

What difference, Gene? It's a beaut.

GENE

> (To SOL)

Why?! You were dead against this march, and suddenly you come up with this! Why?!

SOL

> (Shrugs)

I changed my mind.

GENE

Crap!

> (To CHAMP)

I don't like this!

> (To SOL)

I'm gonna say something! I'm gonna say it to your face! I don't think you are who you say you are! I think you're something else!

...

CHAMP

Gene…

SOL

You're right. I'm not Jewish. My father was a steelworker in
Youngstown, Ohio…

GENE

(To CHAMP, pointing to the flag)
I think this is a trap! I think this is what they want us to do! And I
can prove it!

(CHAMP considers this. GENE turns to SOL.)
Are you going to march with us?!

SOL

If I feel like it.

GENE

(To CHAMP and JOE)
You hear that?! If he feels like it!

(To SOL)
In case you don't remember, pal, this club voted on it!
Unanimously! You have to march!

SOL

No, I don't.

GENE

Okay!

(To CHAMP)
I want this man brought up on charges! For violating club
discipline … ! And democratic centralism! And,uh, conspiring
with the enemy and for … being an FBI informant, sent here to
lead us into this terrible trap!

JOE

(Wan but urgent)

JOE(CONT'D)

Right. It is a trap. They're going to laugh at us as we march up the aisle to discredit us, then they're going to kill us, and if they do that there won't be any club left, and how can we continue our work then?

SOL

That could be. But if you kick me out, that loses you twenty-five percent of your club membership. It also makes one less marcher.

GENE

He's not going to march anyhow! Champ, kick him out and call off the march!

JOE
(Stands, wobbly)

Yes!
(THEY ALL look to CHAMP for leadership.)

CHAMP

No! We're going to need everyone! We're going to march! Not only are we going to march, but we're going to march and sing "The Internationale"!
(JOE sinks back on his cot, his hand on his head.)

BLACKOUT.

Lights up on:

Living room Late that night.

(JOE lies in bed in the darkness. SOL enters from the hallway in his
skivvies, the perennial glass in hand, as JOE's radio softly plays, "You'll Never Walk Alone".)

                    SOL
          (From the doorway)
Hey, kid.

                    JOE
What?

                    SOL
Sleeping?

                    JOE
No.

                    SOL
What're you doing?

                    JOE
Reviewing my life.
          (SOL moves to near the bed, sits in a chair.)

                    SOL
Sounds deep.

                    JOE
Actually, every time it leads up to tomorrow and my death. One
time a club splits my skull open. The next time a knife in my
heart. Then guys kicking my kidneys to pieces. The ways are
infinite.

                    SOL
Well...If I was Gene I could tell you not to worry.

                    JOE
That's what's got me worried. He's not saying it anymore.

                    SOL
          (Chuckles lowly)

Yeah, the Old Answer Man finally ran out. Now there's nothing between him and tomorrow but time, and time leaks out. And for their night's pleasure they get to listen to The Hope of the Future boffing each other in the back room.

JOE

Yeah,I thought she was going to kill him,when he finally told her.

SOL

She was some hot breeze she flew out of here.

JOE

I guess they made up.

SOL

Yeah. They can't afford not to. They're the only two perfect people in the world. So, she criticized him severely, and he chewed down some humble pie, and in no time at all they were back to humping for all mankind. And enjoying it more, I think, because they know old Gino's listening and gnashing his teeth. Poor bastard.

JOE

Poor bastard? I thought you hated him.

SOL

No. I just like to tease him. He's such a good soldier. Always self-improving. Correcting his faults like a good Communist.

JOE

And you?

SOL

Me? I'm bigoted, mean and selfish and accept it totally.

                                JOE

Like a good Communist?

                                SOL

No, just an old one.
                (HE laughs)
Listen to that. I'm only thirty-two, but I've been in the movement
eighteen years. I could tell you stories, boy...
                (HE shakes his head in wonder.)

                                JOE

Tell me.
                (SOL studies the boyish face before him, nods in
wistful remembrance.
SOL shrugs.)

                                SOL

Naahh...

                                JOE

No, come on. Tell me

                                SOL

In 1936 I was the youngest member of the American Communist
Party. I was fourteen. Those were great days in Chicago. Just a
kid, but I ran the kitchen in the International Harvester strike. I
fed a thousand people a day, workers and their families. Farmers
from as far south as Cairo slipped through the police blockades
to bring us food. When the company goons tried to break up
the kitchen, they fought alongside us. I remember them; Dan
McCutcheon, Ernst Gorsche, Mollie Dayton.
They weren't Communists, just good people. We loved each other
like brothers and sisters. Man, I thought, this is what Socialism's
going to be like.

JOE

Yeah, I feel like that sometimes, too, with you guys. The whole thing of really being together with people. The kind of feeling you never got with your own family. Solid... Solidarity...

(HE sees that HE has lost the OLDER MAN'S agreement. HE stops. A pause.)

Why'd you get us the flag?

SOL

(Shrugs)

I felt like it

JOE

Are you going to march with us tomorrow?

(SOL says nothing, but levels JOE with a look of wistful longing.)

You really should, you know. I mean, since you caused it to happen.

SOL

(Smiles gently)

Don't think so much. That's what Gennadi always said to me. Things happen. What can you do?

(Takes a drink)

Here's a funny story. During the war they're unloading a lend-lease freighter from the U.S. in Murmansk. From the forehold they're offloading cases of machine guns and Spam for the Soviet Army. From the afthold they're bringing out cases of Scotch and canned vegetables. Understand, during the war there was no such thing as vegetables in all the Soviet Union. Precious as gold. Back from the afthold for two blocks a line of staff cars, coming in one at a time to load up with the good stuff. Cars with insignias of Generals, Admirals. Down at the other end the guards catch one of the dock workers with a can of Spam in his pocket. They walk him over to the wall of the shed and shoot him dead. When asked why, they say they're cracking down on theft.

(JOE is not sure HE's heard the punch line, or if HE has, where the joke lies.)

Get it? Cracking down on theft? Don't you think that's funny?

                    JOE

No. It's awful.

                    SOL

You're right. It is.

                    JOE

It's also anti-Soviet.

                    SOL

Right. I'll never tell it again.
          (Nods down toward his crotch)
Should I examine myself self-critically?

                    JOE
          (Doesn't smile)
Why did you tell me that?
                    SOL
          (Thinks, then)
What if I told you I saw it? Would you believe me?

                    JOE
          (Studies SOL, dubious)
Well, I don't know...

                    SOL

In that case, I didn't see it. I made it up.
          (A Silence, as SOL falls into a remembrance.)

                    JOE

You haven't answered my question..

                    SOL

Which question was that?

                    JOE

Are you gonna march?

SOL

(Drinks, thinks)

That would be fun, eh? Marching again, chest out, head high, proclaiming the future.

(Mock belief, sings)

"Fly higher and higher and higher,
Our emblem is the Soviet star..."

(HE falls silent for a moment.)

I haven't proclaimed the future much lately. I wonder how it would feel. I haven't been beaten up in...Jesus, years. The last time was, let's see...Galveston, 1943. Almost ten years. I'm out of practice. You can always tell when the Party's made a wrong decision. We stop getting beat up.

JOE

Which makes what we're doing tomorrow very right, huh?

SOL

Listen. So you take a beating. A few weeks in the hospital, and you come out and show the girls your scars and get laid all through the Movement.

(JOE looks away, dealing with his fear.)

Or you can duck tomorrow. Show up sick.

(JOE shakes his head, no.)

Why not? Who gives a damn? So it's one less body. With the adults there, there'll still be five. That's respectable.

JOE

I couldn't let the guys down.

SOL

What guys? Champ? He's so deep in his own movie, he won't know if you're there or not. Gene? He'd love to duck himself. And he would if Champ wasn't leading the charge.

JOE

I just couldn't face myself.

                              SOL
                    (Studies him)
Don't think so much, March or don't march. It doesn't matter.
That's the point. Nothing anyone does matters that much. There's
no great help...and no great hurt.

                              JOE
                    (caught by this last)
No? You mean informing doesn't hurt?

                              SOL
                    (Smiles enigmatically)
It's all a dance. We do one step, the Soviets another. We dance
around and dance around and the only people who get hurt are
the poor, and who gives a shit about them anyhow?
                    (JOE is studying him)
Listen, I'll tell you a secret. The FBI is keeping the Party alive.

                              JOE
                    (Laughs)
What?

                              SOL
Listen, now. If the Party died of its own stupidity, which it would
if left to its own devices, who would the Feebies have to hold up
as the Great Red Menace? When they went to Congress to get
their appropriation every year, who could they point to as the
"great threat to the American Way of Life"? A third of the dues
of the American Communist Party are being paid by Mr. J. Edgar
Hoover. Informers.

                              JOE
Uh-huh.

                              SOL
It's all a dance.

                              JOE

Why are you doing it?

                              SOL
                      (shrugs helplessly)
Why not? It's four hundred a month. Tax free.

                              JOE

But...you could go away. Start a new life.

                              SOL

                      (Wistful smile)
         Where? The Movement's all I know. All my friends
are here. If I didn't have my friends to inform on, what would I
have? (JOE regards him with pity and contempt.)

                              SOL

Are you gonna tell on me?
                      (JOE turns away, troubled.)
It's all right, if you feel you have to.
                      (HE rises, crosses to the door.)
Know what I love about you, kid? You don't know what you
believe in, but you're a believer.
                      (HE exits. From Offstage, a sardonic call)
March, two, three- "Fly higher and higher and higher..."
                      (And JOE is left to deal with more demons than
before.)

         BLACKOUT.

         LIGHTS: up on

         The shop. "Red Square."

         (The conveyor belt runs at a brisk pace, carrying
its monotonous load of car hoods Onstage and then Off.

                              182

The sounds of the factory running at full tilt. Then
the lunch bell rings. Suddenly all is silence. The
conveyor stops a hood
in mid-air. Everything hangs in stillness for a long
moment. Then, from the far end of the shop can be
heard the faint sound of MALE VOICES,very few.)

OUR BOYS

"Arise, ye prisoners of starvation,
Arise, ye wretched of the earth..."
(The singing grows slowly louder and more
confident. It is joined now by
a low murmuring sound that grows with it, until the two seem to
climax in an outburst of yells and melee.Shouts and curses and
grunts of pain.These continue, then JOE appears, half dragging
GENE Onstage and toward the pallets and stacks. One arm hangs
limp at JOE's side. His face is covered with blood. GENE drags one
leg and cradles one arm, broken, with the other, but has no blood
on him.)

JOE
(In full roar)
Did you see me clip that guy?! Full in the fucking face?! See the
blood?! A fucking gusher!
GENE
Get Champ! ...
JOE
...And the other guy?! I got him right in the balls! I crossed his
fucking eyes for him! ...
(HE lowers GENE to the pallet, then goes over to
the trash pile, looking for something.)

GENE
Get Champ out of there! ...

183

JOE

Right there...

GENE

They're killing him! ...

JOE

(Looking, testing sticks with his one good arm)
No, no, he's doing good! He's got that flag pole! He's fucking
spearing guys with it!

(HE picks up a stickand strikes a pallet, breaking
the stick. HE throws it down.)

GENE

Hurry!

JOE

I love it! I fucking love it! Didja see me?! Before we started I
almost fainted! I barfed twice, and then we started! And there
was something in me! I grew! I saw fucking Atlas, big as the
world! I wanted those guys! I saw them coming and I wanted
them! Eat 'em fucking alive! Beat their fucking brains in!

GENE

Joe, stop! You're crazy! Get Champ! ...

JOE

Did you see Keller?! He was watching me! Goddamn right, Keller!
You're looking at a killer!

(Giggles)

Oh, god, am I alive! If my old man could see me now! Haaa-haaaa!
Fuck reason! Kill the bastards! ...Ha-haaa! Under every liberal, a
fucking killer! ....

GENE

What are you doing?! ....

JOE

I need a bat! A club! Did you see Sol?! Jesus, he marched! Crazy,
man! I never thought he would!

GENE

He went down....!

JOE

You saw him?! ...

GENE

I think, yes...! Joe, hurry!
          (JOE lifts up a three-inch round wooden dowel,
two feet long, hefts it.)

JOE

Got it! Oh, man! Gonna bust me some heads now!

GENE

Get Champ...

JOE

          (ignoring him, as HE goes back into fray, one arm
hanging)
You cocksuckers! Watch your asses! This is one Jew who kills!
          (HE exits. GENE sits there, half-leaning against the
stack.)

GENE

Insane! ... All crazy! ... God, what are we doing?! ...
          (A wrench in his stomach causes him to wretch.
Blood comes out of his mouth. HE touches it, examines it.)
God, am I dying?!
          (Tears come to his eyes.)
Not like this! ... Not yet! ...
          (In a wail of yearning)
Oh, Champ! Champ! I'm so ashamed! ...

BLACKOUT.

Lights up on:

The house. A week later. Morning.

(JOE, one arm in a sling, a bandage over one ear, goes through a carton
examining objects. A radio plays"Rawhide" sung by Frankie Laine.)

GENE (offstage)
You just asked to see him and they let you?

JOE
Yeah.

GENE (offstage)
He didn't have family?

JOE
I guess not. They had me identify him.

GENE (offstage)
What did he look like?

JOE
Dead.
(GENE appears at the door with clothes folded over his arm. His other arm is in a cast, as is his lower leg.)

GENE
Mmm, dead people ... Don't have much energy. Tend to lie around a lot.

                          JOE
            (Looks at him)
Smarmy, Gino. You asked a question...

                          GENE
So answer it...!

                          JOE
What are you so snappish about...?

                          GENE
I'm not! Was he bruised, bashed in? What?!

                          JOE
Not bashed in. He had a bruise on the side of the face and the
little hole in his temple where the nail went in.

                          GENE
Jesus...

                          JOE
The doctor said it was a hundred-to-one shot.

                          GENE
            (Puts down clothes)
Well, I never liked the man, but I never wished him that.

                          JOE
            (Sighs)
Yeah.
                          GENE
Isn't it funny? After all our suspicions, he died a hero's death.
Some guys have all the luck.

                          JOE
Yeah.

GENE
(Hobbles offstage to SOL's room again)
I mean, he wasn't lucky to die, but if you have to go, that's the
way. Did you see the front page of <u>The Worker</u>? "Working-Class
Martyr." Shit, for that fat slob. And the <u>PW</u>? "He Died For Peace
And Friendship." The creep, he'd died for a piece of bacon! Who
ever thought he'd march?! What the hell was he doing there?!

JOE
(Looking at a photo)
I guess he wanted to...
(Decides not to say it)
I don't know)
(GENE reappears with some shoes, starts putting
them in a carton.)

GENE
(Muttering)
You work your whole life, and then along comes a grabayun like
that and takes it all. A big memorial at the Unitarian Church.
There'll be thousands there. Pete Seeger's coming in to sing. Even
the bourgeois press is going to cover it.
(HE exits Offstage again)
Labor's first martyr since Tom Mooney. That fat fuck!
(More quietly)
Don't mean to speak ill of the dead, but...
(Sighs)
Never mind.
(HE returns with a handful of pens, rulers, erasers,
and the like, in one hand. In the other HE holds up a half-used
bottle of mayonnaise and a spoon.)
Sol Binder to the end. He ate mayonnaise straight.
(HE throws it all in the box.)

JOE
Look at this.

JOE(CONT'D)
(HE goes to GENE, shows him the photo)
He was in the Soviet Union. He said something about...
(HE turns the photo over, reads)
"Lend-lease, 1943, Murmansk. Lieutenant Gennadi Semyanov ... "

GENE
Must've been in the Merchant Marine ...
JOE
(Turns the photo back over)
A bottle of Scotch ...
GENE
What?
JOE
The bottle they're holding between them ...

GENE
Scotch? In the Soviet Union? I doubt it. Probably some local hootch.

JOE
(Crosses back, tosses photo in box)
Yeah. Probably.
(He surveys the clothes and boxes, paucious as they are.)
Is that it?
GENE
He didn't have much.
JOE
So, what do we do with it?
GENE
Hank'll take it with her. The PW's going to have a fundraiser Sunday. They're going to auction it off. Holy relics of the First Church of Christ Communist.

JOE
Well, he did die for it.

GENE

Here they come.
>(They watch.)

JOE

He doesn't look bad.

GENE
>(In private agony)
No.
>(The front door opens and CHAMP enters, aided
by HANK. HE is bandaged around his head, has one arm in a sling
and one leg in a cast to the hip.)
Well, the conquering hero home at last.
>(HE embraces CHAMP, as does JOE after him.)
How're you feeling?

CHAMP

Fine! Fine! A little giddy, but fine!

HANK
>(A bit severely)
He's supposed to rest.

CHAMP

I will, hon, I will ...

JOE

Well, you look fine ...

HANK
>(Surveying the cast and bandages of white)
Lord, look at all of you.
>(And THEY do for a silent moment, the survivors)

                    JOE

Well, we made it!

                   GENE

Unbeaten, and unbowed!

                  CHAMP

Not unbeaten.

                   GENE

Right!Beaten but unbowed!

                    JOE

They couldn't kill us!
            (Looks to the boxes and clothes)
Well, most of us ... We won!
            (And the THREE CRIPPLES dance around in a
limping, dipping, jerky celebration, till CHAMP stops them.)

                  CHAMP

Comrades. We have to talk.

                   HANK

Comrade, why don't you take your nap first? The comrades will
wait.

                 JOE & GENE

Sure, sure. Champ, get some rest.

                  CHAMP

I've been resting all week. There's work to be done. Plans to be
made. Evaluations.
            (They all hobble and dodder into seats, emitting
little grunts of pain with every move.)
I don't know if you know, but I've been asked to speak at Sol's
memorial. I want to deliver the greetings of all industrial clubs
to that gathering. I want to convey to them our grief and our
redoubled dedication to follow in the footsteps of that son of the
working class, our comrade, Solomon Binder.
            (GENE sighs in repressed torment.)

CHAMP(CONT'D)

I want to assure them that, just as this young man, well, this man, stepped forward to offer his life for the cause of peace, with his last breaths facing the blows of the warmongers. We vow to do the same.

(His emotion growing, and GENE sighing)

In his name I'm going to call for an end to the war in Korea.!
Let his life be our beacon! And his death our rallying cry!
Peace!Troops home now!

(HE finishes, waits. There is a hush)

How is that?

HANK

Very moving.

GENE

(Biting his lip)

Mmm.

JOE

Well ... I'm all for Solly becoming a hero, but I'd hate for it to blow up in our faces ... The night before the march he admitted to me he was a government informer.

(THEY all gasp)

ALL

What?! He did?! Oh, my!

GENE

I knew it!

(HE punches the air with his fist)

I knew it!

(HE cries out in pain, as his arm is moved)

Aaagh!

(Happy tears from his eyes)

I was right! Ha-haaa! The fat fart was a traitor! No one who hides mayonnaise could be a hero!

HANK

Oh, dear.
(To JOE)
Why didn't you tell anyone?

JOE

(Shrugs)
I was brought up not to tell on people.

CHAMP

But informing on an informer is not informing!
(He winces from moving too much)
If you'd told us, we might've done something!

JOE

What? It was hours before the march.

CHAMP

Stopped him from marching!

JOE

How?! It's a free country. He had a right to march!

GENE

Ah, I love it! Whatever comes of my life, I'm vindicated! That little scumsucker gets exposed for the rotten leech he was! A press conference! We call a press conference! Ow! The press, TV, everyone!

CHAMP

Whoa ... Whoa, whoa, whoa! Hold on there!
(More calmly)
Let's look at this objectively. This guy has become a national figure. There's a police investigation going on into his death. Memorials all over the country ...

HANK

... At a time when the movement needs a hero desperately ...

CHAMP

... If we expose him, what's that going to do to morale?

JOE

But if the FBI exposes him as one of their own, is that good for us?

GENE
(Rises, painfully)
No! We have to expose him! Tell it all! His gluttony! His raucous drunkenness! His racism! Defeatism! Revisionism! Adventurism! Owww!
(His pain pushes him down into his seat)

HANK

Wait, now. Why should the FBI say anything? He was marching with us. He gave his life for us. How do they explain that?

CHAMP
(Points to HANK, admiringly)
The voice of leadership.
GENE
(Desperate)
He didn't march for us! He was probably so drunk he forgot which side he was on and fell in with us!
CHAMP
Calmer heads, Gene. We're dealing here with the fate of a national movement ...

GENE

What national movement, for Christ's sake?! A few thousand people all told! ...

HANK

... Which is more than the Bolsheviks had in Russia on the eve of the Revolution ...

GENE

Oh, my god, an analogy! Is our land overrun with Germans?! Are we starving and no factories running ?! Do our farmers have nowhere to sell their crops?! Expose the prick and let me die in peace!

CHAMP

(Quietly but firmly)

Now, Gene, I know you had differences with the man. I wasn't too crazy about him myself. But this is beyond that. Sometimes you have to do things for the good of the Movement. If we four have to live with the small irony that this Communist martyr was in fact a government fink, well, I'm sure there are bigger ironies in life. I'm going to call a vote. All those for preserving the unity of the Party and the Movement by martyrizing Solomon Binder say "aye."

HANK

Aye.

JOE

(Sighs)

Aye.

CHAMP

Aye.

(THEY all look to GENE)

GENE

(Slumps visibly)

Oh, shit. Unanimous.

CHAMP

Okay. Great.

HANK

I just want to say, they don't know it yet, but when the true workers' history comes out, the people of the world will thank you for your vote.

CHAMP

Okay. I just want to make one comment on the march itself. I thought we all did really well. I want to single out Joe Morris for courage above and beyond. But I have to point our that you went a little overboard. You left me unprotected to go chase one of Parker's men into the stacks, just to, as you said then, "bash his fucking head in." I mean, I appreciate your zeal, but ... As you were bashing his head in, they were bashing mine. You got a little carried away.

JOE

I know. I lost control. Frankly, I'm appalled at my own violence.

CHAMP

No, no. Rage is good. But make it socially productive. Okay? Okay. Good meeting. Anything else?

(A pause, then)

GENE

I'm queer.

HANK

What? You don't feel well?

GENE

No, queer. Homosexual. A fairy.

CHAMP

What are you talking about?

GENE

I've known it for some time. It's why I had to leave Harvard. I've tried to master it with Marxist-Leninist discipline, but it's no good.

GENE(CONT'D)
(HE turns to CHAMP)
I love you. I understand it's in a way I know is wrong, but I can't help it. I've been going up to Hollywood to ease the pain, but it doesn't work ... I've been endangering the club, because if the FBI ever caught me at it, they'd blackmail me into becoming an informer. I mean, if the Irving Feibel exposé damn near did us in, what would a photo of me kissing something I shouldn't be kissing do?

HANK
You're in love with Irving, I mean, Champ? My Champ?

CHAMP
You love me ... that way?
(GENE nods, yes)
But ... that's impossible. I'm engaged to Hank. I mean, Communists aren't queers.

GENE
This one is. I've been in the Movement all my life. I don't know what I'll do, but I'm going away.
JOE
Gene, Geez, this is terrible. I mean, if you go away.

CHAMP
It is. If you go away, we've lost half our membership.

GENE
I'm sorry.

HANK
Maybe if we had some discussion, we could get to the root of it and cure it. It's a sickness, you know, like pneumonia.

GENE
Do pneumonia victims get a yen for big, blond men?

CHAMP

That is sick. I'm really shocked, Gene.

      (Sweat pours from his brow. HE wipes it with his good hand)

I've always thought of you as a comrade. To think that all this time, you were thinking of me as ... Is it warm in here?

      (HANK goes, opens a window)

Well, what are we going to do about it? The club, that is, what is the club going to do?

JOE

      (To GENE)

Can you go to a doctor or something?

GENE

I did. He basically told me to pull myself together. I tried. No, there's no other way. You have to expel me, pass the word that no one is to talk to me, that I'm cast out. Isn't that what happens, Hank?

HANK

Yes, I'm afraid so.

      (A depressed silence)

JOE

Jesus, what a club. A martyred FBI stoolie, a Jew posing as a Gentile, a Communist fairy, and a violent maniac. Now I know what I'm doing here. I found the jury of my peers. But god, how are the likes of us going to make Socialism?

      (THEY think about it)

CHAMP

True.

      (Reaches down, finds something)

But we did march.

                    JOE

Yes, we did.

                    GENE

Crazy as it was ...

                    CHAMP

And what lesson can we draw from it?

                    JOE

Don't ever, ever do it again.

                    CHAMP

No, not that. Look around you. Whatever we are individually,
however weak or confused we are, when we band together under
our Communist banner, we are strong ...
          (The OTHERS are less enthused)
That is the strength of our Movement. That is the ...

          (There is a knock at the back door)

                    JOE

The back door.

                    GENE

I'll get it.
          (HE goes out. CHAMP and HANK rise to see who is
coming. To EVERYONE's surprise, GENE leads in KELLER)

                    KELLER

Hey, all.
          (To JOE)
Hey, killer.
          (To CHAMP)
Captain Midnight.
          (To HANK)

KELLER(CONT'D)

Hi, My name's Keith Keller.
> (To ALL)

I woulda come in the front door, but I know who you got out there.

CHAMP

How did you know where we live?

KELLER

You're in the phone book.

CHAMP

Oh, right.

JOE

What can we do for you?

KELLER

Oh, nothing. Just driving around. You know, you guys are Daffy Duck as far as Communism is concerned, but I gotta hand it to ya, you got guts.
> (A skeptical silence greets him)

I fought in Korea, you know. I don't care for the Russkies too much.

CHAMP

Well, we do.

KELLER

I know.
> (An awkward silence, then KELLER turns to JOE)

I read The Fountainhead. Ever read that?

JOE

Uh, actually, no.
> (Another pause)

KELLER

I believe in what I fought for, but ... It weren't that great over there. It don't do you much good seeing your friends die. Well, you know that.

HANK

We do.

KELLER

I ... just dropped by ...

CHAMP

Okay.

HANK

Why don't we sit? Would you like a beer?

KELLER

Uh ... fine.
                (THEY resume seats, as JOE gimps out for the
beer.)

CHAMP

How long you been in the shop?

KELLER

Almost a year. I'd be off the line by now, but I don't get along with my foreman.

GENE

Who's that? Roby?

                (JOE brings him the beer)

KELLER

Thank you. I always tell him when the line's speeding up. He don't appreciate that. Boys on the line tell me to shut up. But ta hell with him. I speak my mind.

JOE

You still going to kill me?

KELLER

Oh, man, I was just joshing with you. I told you, I admire Jewish people. They know how to get things done.

     (The OTHERS scrutinize him for a long moment. An urging look from HANK to CHAMP)

CHAMP

     (Carefully)
Tell me, how do you feel about the union?

KELLER

     (Thinks)
It's okay.

GENE

Uh-huh. And, uh, what about its various committees?

KELLER

Well, I don't know much about them.

JOE

Ah-hah.

CHAMP

How ... do you feel about Negroes?

KELLER

     (Thinks long and deep)
Nee-groes. Let's see ...
     (THEY await his answer as ...)

LIGHTS:Fade to

BLACKOUT

END OF PLAY

THE DEFENSE OF TAIPEI

BY

CONRAD BROMBERG

CAST OF CHARACTERS

DON, a white man in his late thirties, falsely young.

AIME, a middle aged black man trying to get along.

JANE, Don's wife, glamorous and porcelain.

VIOLA, Aime's wife, a young black matron.

SETTINGS

ACT I: A sterile TV studio

ACT II: Don's home
Scene 1:

ACT II: Aime's home
Scene 2:

ACT II: The TV studio

TIME

Two consecutive days in history

PLACE

America

ACT I

SCENE: A television studio room. On stage left wall are various colored signal lights, shots and mechanism. Against stage right wall rests a large metal closet, taller than a man, from which props are taken. The upstage wall is bare. Two straight back chairs are faced out from it. A circle is marked off from the center of the room, the playing area. The control booth is out in the audience. As in such places there is no sense of time, only artificial light and the ordered civility of an IBM civilization.

AT RISE: (AIME sits on the stage right chair. He is preoccupied. DON paces back and forth across the room. HE eyes AIME, then approaches him.)

DON

Are you alright?

(AIME nods)

Something on your mind?

AIME
(Shakes his head)

The last scene we did reminded of something, my boy.

DON

Oh. I am going to tell you something. You have to keep it under your hat, though, away from them.
(Nods his head toward the control booth out front)
Are you listening? Can I trust you?

(AIME nods)

I like to break wind in bed. Well?

AIME

That is really something.

DON

My wife doesn't say a word. Just sleeps in the other room for
a month. I would rather she shouted or threatened to tell on
me. She won't, though. My wife is a very rational person. She
thinks I'm being hostile. Not at all. It simply comes over me. Not
the physical urge, but the overwhelming need to express my
individuality. Do you see my point? Today everyone goes around
agreeing with everyone. That's fine, and proves how well we
have solved the problems of life, death, poverty, hate, etc. But
truthfully, and I don't mean this as a criticism, if everyone in
the room is saying yes, after a while it is hard to tell one person
from another. Do you see? Sometimes, in order to assert your
individuality, there's the need to say no. Can't you see it? Late at
night, the bedroom dark, then suddenly...
        (HE gestures the silent sound of WHAM, the shock
of it)
What a great way to say no! I tell you, the power surges through
my veins! I feel myself, so present! Of course, it wears off after an
hour or so, but for that time... what self!

AIME

Isn't that something.

DON

What are you thinking?

AIME

Nothing. Not a thing.

DON

You wouldn't be thinking of using that information
        (Nods toward the control booth)
Would you?

                    AIME

Why would I want to do that?

                    DON

To get in good with them and put me in the pan all at once? You
know that is impossible, don't you? They only listen to me. But to
make sure, you tell me something about yourself, something you
do.

                    AIME

I don't do anything.

                    DON

Everybody does something.

                    AIME

I... I pee in the middle of the bowl where there is company in the
next room.
                    DON

So they can hear it.

                    AIME

It sounds like a thousand waterfalls!

                    DON

Right in the deep water?

                    AIME

Sometimes I orchestrate it out to the side or in to the center. But
I always have to be careful. If it grows too fortissimo, it carries up
to the neighbors.

                    DON

Were you ever caught?

AIME

No, but I know they would report me.

DON

What does your wife say?

AIME

She... she calls me a savage and... reminds me we left all that behind in the jungle.

DON

A savage...

AIME

She is perfectly right.

DON

A savage... I hear that anyone caught is brought into a room with a big black chair with wires.

AIME

And then what?

DON

I don't know.

AIME

I hear that anyone is strapped to a white marble slap with a trough at the foot.

DON

And then what?

AIME

I don't know... Is that what they do here when you get a blue light?

DON

And then they tilt the slap feet down?

AIME

And drain it into a trough?

DON

A blue light offense is the worst.

AIME

Have you heard the screams?

DON

No screams. Once, before you were here they flicked the wrong switch and I heard it over that.
                    (Points to a PA system on wall, stage left)

AIME

The same one the music comes from. What was the sound?

DON

Whoever it was, asked, "What is being done to me? Am I allowed to ask what is being done to me?"

AIME

And then what?
                    (DON gestures–nothing)
It's not a blue light offense to do that in the middle of the bowl.

DON

Or to do that in bed.
                    AIME

Is it?
DON
Is it?!

                    (This NEXT SECTION THEY direct indirectly out toward the control booth)

AIME

It's really not more than a boyish prank.

DON

It reminds me of my days in boy's camp.

AIME

It isn't as if you ask embarrassing questions? Or anything like that.

DON

They know you mean no harm by it.

AIME

Nor do you.

DON

I don't do it often.

AIME

Nor do I. Once a month.

DON

I doubt if I do it once every two months.

AIME

What I meant was once a month in the warm season. In the cold season I don't do it more than once every six months, which averages out to once every three months.

DON

You always have to best me, don't you. If I say two, you say three. If I fart, you pee. Boy, are you competitive!

AIME

(Whispers fearfully)

I didn't mean it that way. What you do is far better than what I do. It is...noisier. It might very well be mistaken for a gunshot. It takes courage to sound like a gunshot.

DON
(Loudly)

Now you are sucking up to me. No, I won't shush! Half the time you are undercutting me with them, the rest you brown-nose me for favors. I should expect that. You have the right color nose to start with. Don't be angry.

AIME

I'm not angry. I like you.

DON

Do you? Not because I am the one who talks to them, who requisitions new scenes?

AIME

I am satisfied with what I have.

DON

Something in the way you say that sends a cold chill through me. I have done my best to befriend you and help you but something in you disapproves of me. You insist on make me uncomfortable. What have I done to you?

AIME

Nothing.

DON

Then why this carping little presence that constantly pulls you back. Not only with me but with all this. Why not a moment ago after the Honest Man scene you scurried back to your chair without a word about what we had just done. Don't you like the scene?

AIME

It's a wonderful scene.

DON

And then sat there with your mind off somewhere thinking God knows what...

AIME

I was thinking about my boy. Something happened to him. They told us this morning. We lost him.

DON

Lost him? How?

AIME

An automobile. The strangest part is, that an hour after they told us he was gone, I couldn't remember his name. A father should be able to remember his son's name. But I can't. It's silly, I know, but it's been bothering me.

DON

I can tell. You are not with the work today.

AIME

I am with it. These scenes are terribly meaningful to me. I...

STEWARDESS' VOICE
(Over PA on left–jet noises behind her)
Good afternoon, ladies and gentlemen, welcome aboard Flight 401 non-stop to Wichita, Sao Paolo, Avignon, Karachi, and Bakersfield. We will be flying under optimum weather conditions at forty thousand feet...

AIME
(At chart schedule)
Isn't it something the way everything comes through this studio? Yes sir, you can sit right here and keep up with everything that's going on out there.
(Laughs self-consciously under DON's suspicious gaze)
I'm with it. I really am.
(DON does not relent. AIME busies himself at chart)
Let's see, the airplane scene... Here it is. The Sole Survivor.

DON

No, no, we do that one later.

AIME

Oh, yes, let's see, our next scene is... Defense of Taipei... ha-ha... I'll get the props. Don't trouble yourself.

(Crosses to closet, pulls out army combat blouses, helmets, and one toy sub- machine gun)
Really something. Science, boy, what would we do without it? I depend on it.

(AIME hands DON a blouse and a helmet. DON takes a real rifle from the closet. As it emerges from the closet, it produces a frozen moment between the two men. THEY resume dressing. AIME puts two chairs in the playing circle, placing them to form a barricade out to the audience. HE falls back into his own thoughts momentarily)
Billy? ... Benjamin?

DON

What?

AIME
(Brought back, smiles)

Nothing.

DON

Check your gun.

(AIME winds spring, pulls trigger, toy sparks and rachety sounds emit from the gun)

AIME

It's fine.

(DON works bolt of rifle. AIME reacts uneasily to it. DON pulls trigger. Gun fires loudly with the sharp crack of a real rifle. AIME flinches as if it's his, then smiles weakly)

DON

What are you thinking?

                    AIME
Nothing.

                    DON
               (Slapping real rifle)
You'd like to have this one wouldn't you? See it open a man's
chest at five hundred yards? Who would you like to see writhing
on the ground?
               (AIME shrugs fearfully)
Who?
                    AIME
Nobody. Really.
                    DON
Sometimes the bullets are real.
                    AIME
Are they real today?
                    DON
I don't know.

        (DON works the bolt again. AIME flinches, smiles
again. The yellow warning lights signal. A silence ensures as the
two men wait in the circle. It becomes oppressive as each is too
paranoically aware of each other)

                    AIME
Ha...

                    DON
Ha ha...

                    AIME
Ha... ha...

        (The red signal flashes. The room is dark now, with
only the circle lit. THEY begin, AIME kneeling behind barricade
and DON looking out over his shoulder)

                    DON
How's it going, Sergeant?

                    AIME
We drove 'em back, sir.

                    DON
Estimated losses.

                    AIME
We mowed 'em down like grass, sir. About five hundred twenty-three of them.

                    DON
They sure don't care about human life, do they? Just keep coming in yellow hordes.

                    AIME
Yes sir, and we keep mowing 'em down like grass.

                    DON
Any of our men get it?

                    AIME
          (Grim)
Yes sir, we lost one man… Swenson.
                    DON
          (Grimmer)
Swenson? … The kid from the farm in Minnesota?

                    AIME
Yes sir, the one who was always writing home to his folks.

                    DON
The one who was always talking about his girl.

                    AIME
Yes sir. Sylvia.
DON
               (a warning look to Aime)
Sorry, er, Sir,uh … Polly Ann.

DON

And this was his last day on the line.

AIME

He was supposed to be shipped home tomorrow?

DON

I told him last night. He asked me not to tell you or any of the men. He said, "I'm here to fight, sir, for as long as I am on Formosa."

AIME

That dumb, brave kid.

DON

He was all soldier.

AIME

Why do they send raw kids like him out here? Kids who never had a chance to live!

DON

Our country is made up of millions of boys just like Swenson. Kids who would rather throw a football than a grenade. Who would rather hold hands with their girl in a movie or putter around with old cars. Kids in letterman sweaters at school proms…Clerking in Dad's drug store after school. Those kids are the bone and fiber of our nation. They know what a good life she has given them, and when she calls, they are ready. To fight, yes, even to die.

AIME
(Wiping one tear)
Yes sir, I know. Just sometimes it gets to you.

I know Sergeant. You're not as tough as you look. Remember this God-forsaken, gook-ridden hill is an outpost of democracy. It's going to stay that way, too. We have the air power! The sea power! The ground power! Plus the intangibles, freedommoralityspirituality...

AIME

(Very Negro, reverent)

Spir-it-u-al-i-ty...

(Off-key bugle sounds)

Here they come again, sir!

DON

What do you say, Sergeant>

AIME

Let 'em come!

(Stands up)

Come on, you yellow sons of Hades! We're ready for you!

(Begins firing)

For Swenson!

DON

(Begins firing as music swells)

And Jones!

AIME

And Guido!

DON

And Rothman!

AIME

You'll never take Taipei!

(THEY stand there, firing, as the music crescendos and ends. A green signal flashes. AIME and DON relax. The room lights come up. THEY replaces the gear in the closet)

A great scene. How long do we plan to hold Taipei?

                    DON

Forever, I imagine.

                    AIME

Forever. What a great word.
          (Starts to cross back to his chair)

                    DON

Forever is the best word in the human language. What do you do
when your wife calls you a savage?

                    AIME

I don't do anything.

                    DON

You do. I can see it in your eyes.

                    AIME

I... I lower my face.

                    DON

You can trust me.

                    AIME

I don't do anything.

                    DON
          (Crosses back to closet)
You do.
          (Takes out a pistol, turns to AIME and works
mechanism)

                    AIME

I... bite her nose

                    DON

Gosh, bite her nose! ... You do more.

                    AIME

My eyes are lying. I...

                    DON

I can always tell when you are holding out on me. You smile sheepishly.

                    AIME

My smile is lying.
          (DON works mechanism, raises gun)
I pull her finger!

                    DON

Pull her finger! Golly!
          (Paces, to himself)
Pull her finger...Bite her nose!
          (Pantomimes the two acts, works the pistol)
Tonight! Tonight, I will definitely do it. She won't catch me this
time! No sir! That is a good expression of yourself, pulling her
finger, but it is nothing compared to what I am going to do!

                    AIME

Surprise your wife?

                    DON

Correct!
          (Works gun excitedly)
I thought of it yesterday. A Modern kitchen. She prepares dinner.
Fully clothed in sweater, skirt, stockings and high heels. But
no underpants. That is important, no panties! The children are
playing in the living room. I sneak in behind her, ready. As she
bends over to put the roast in the oven, I... what do you think?

                    222

                    AIME
          (Uneasy)
Very good.

                    DON
Think of the shock! She might very well drop the roast and ask
who it is.

                    AIME
She would, she would.

                    DON
Think of the risk. The children might come in for peanut butter
and jelly. My timing might be off. If I catch her off balance I topple
into the roast and sold my pants. Then she turns to me the way
she does and says
          (Innocently)
"What are you doing?" What can I say to that? I am foolish,
incompetent, crude... Isn't it a good risk?

                    AIME
Very good.

                    DON
Say the whole thing.

                    AIME
Your risk is very good.

                    DON
Substitute beautiful for good.

                    AIME
Your risk is very beautiful.

                    DON
Yes, yes. Now my individuality.

                              AIME

You are very individual.

                              DON

Use unique in a sentence.

                              AIME

You individuality is unique.

                              DON
                    (Alone, filled)
Yes! That is the seed of greatness! I have great deeds in my heart!
They need only to be awakened! To rise and, like a colossus,
bestride the world in the service of my country. Me and my
country, growing, swelling, increasing and increasing!

            (The two are alone in their thoughts)

                              DON
Aime?
                              AIME
Yes?
                              DON
What a strange name. Is it French?

                              AIME
Yes.

                              DON

Are you French?

                              AIME
No, but somebody was somewhere back in time. The name was
passed down from dying hand to young hand.

                              DON

What did you do as a child?

                              AIME

Worked in a tobacco field.

                              DON

Worked? Is that all?

                              AIME

When the sun went down I sang in church with the others. We
sang out into the darkness outside.
                              DON

Why did you do that?
                              AIME

Dark people sing into darkness to see if they will be answered.

                              DON

Did an answer come back from it?

                              AIME

Only the sun coming back up on the fields.

                              DON

What did you do in your teens?

                              AIME

Worked in a belt factory.
                              DON

And at night?
                              AIME

Walked the streets, stood on corners, waited.

                              DON

Waited for what?

                    AIME
Waited for something to happen.
                    DON
Did something happen?

                    AIME
Only the sun coming back up on the factory walls.

                    DON
And then you came here…

                    AIME
As a janitor.

                    DON
And after a while you were promoted to work with me.

                    AIME
After years, yes.

                    DON
You have done a lot, haven't you?

                    AIME
I had to do a lot.
                    DON
               (A moment of silence)
We have never talked like this, have we?

                    AIME
No, we haven't.
                    DON
Would you tell me some more?

AIME

I was married in Zion Church. I waited with the others for work
on the corner of Tenth and Jefferson. I was cut in the stomach in
Don's Paradise Bar over a woman. I listened to jazz and popped
my fingers in Rick's Record Store. No more though. I used to
drink wine with Fred and Bubber up at his place... No more,
though. I talked race with Arthur, also at the Paradise. No more,
though. Viola, my wife, and I also used to sit on the roof and
watch the stars.

DON

It is amazing! When I feel strong like this I could listen to you all day.
        (Crosses to AIME)
Aime, do you think it is wrong of me to want to surprise my wife.
She doesn't like it, you know. She is very controlled. She used to
like it. When we were young on the beach at night I would do it
and she would laugh out loud and throw her arms around me
and say, " You are marvelous. I never know what to expect from
you next. You are so alive"...I did things in those days.

AIME

My wife and I... Go on.

DON

Well, then I graduated school and came here and... We have
both settled down considerably. That is only natural. We aren't
children anymore.

AIME

That is exactly what I told him.
                    DON

Told who?
                    AIME

My boy, the one we lost. He was always after me about why we
left Washington Avenue to come here with them. I told him, boy,
we can't stay children forever.

DON

Children are always dissatisfied no matter what you tell them. I know I was. I was pretty wild when I was a kid, yelling at school principals and protesting all kinds of things. I was always trying to figure things out, to find the sense in the world. I thought I could make it make sense. I did insane things then. I thought I could beat anything. I was even in a political demonstration.

AIME

Did you win your point?

DON

(Evasively crosses away)

I came here shortly after. Here you can count on things; let's face it, a man can't go around having nothing to count on. He'd go insane.

AIME

Did you win?

DON

Why did you ask that?

AIME

I don't know.

DON

Why are you looking at me that way?

AIME

I'm not looking at you any way.

DON

I lost my good feeling for a moment.
(After a silence)

AIME

Don?

DON

Yes?

AIME

What you said before about making sense of the world? Well, I have a problem about it...

DON

Why? Here we have made the world make sense.

AIME

Yes, and I'm grateful to be here, but... Well... he questioned it.

DON

Who did?

AIME

My child. The one we lost.

DON

Your child?

AIME

I told you, I lost my boy this morning.

DON

Do you have a boy? I have a boy. How old is yours?

AIME

He was nine until this morning. I guess he is still nine, always will be nine.

DON

I never lose my boy. How did you lose yours?

229

AIME

I told you, an automobile.

DON

Did you tell me? I guess I forgot.

AIME

At any rate, I have a problem about him. You see…
                    (Rises, paces)
How can I explain? It has to do with what my life has been. And…
my nature. My name is Aime, which means love. My mother gave
me that name in the shack on the afternoon of my birth. She gave
me that name because the sun shone so angrily that day she feared
I might take in its rays and be an angry child. She told me to live
in love and to seal it she pressed the book of love to my infant lips.
But the room was so dark she gave me another name, Sojourner,
which means searcher. She told me journey in search. To seal it she
pressed her open eyes to my lips. Since then I have been condemned
to journey in her ways. I say condemned, because the way of the
world is murder and ignorance and I have journeyed through both.
When that man's knife burned by belly, I wondered if his way might
not be away . When I took a woman to my room, in the middle of my
scream I asked myself might not her way be the answer. Or when I
sank into my wine dream, and later when wine was not enough, into
my dope dream, I wondered if they might be the path to meaning.
They proved false. So I married and begot children and worked (I
have always worked) and stood before white buildings. One day the
door of one of those buildings opened and admitted me alone. As I
stood in the great marble rotunda, I knew I had arrived. My journey
was over. This was the hall of meaning. I came to you and gave
myself to you. I learned to speak as you, to dress as you do, to think
as you do.

DON

We have the answers.

AIME

I believe it. I want to believe it. But then my first and only child grew to be strange. He planted poisoned questions in my brain. Questions about you, about all of this.

DON

Questions? About what?

AIME

Well...

(Takes the leap)

For one about the scene we just did.

DON

The Defense of Taipei? What did he say?

AIME

Well... he implied that possibly the scene wasn't completely truthful about what was going on in the real battle over there. That... and of course I reject the idea...that possibly we might not be able to hold Taipei forever.

DON

No wonder you lost him. That's pretty treacherous thinking, even for a child...

AIME

I agree. You don't know how I warned him, punished him for it.

DON

Besides, the thought is ridiculous. We have the air power, the sea power, the ground power...

AIME

....Plus those great intangibles, I know, and I would dismiss him and his questions, except that... he was such a strange boy. He had some power over people. Some strange knowledge that

AIME(CONT'D)

made people either hate him… or follow him. He would vanish for weeks at a time. When he returned I would ask him, where did you go? You were gone a week… I walked, walked and talked. Who did you talk to? … People… I didn't expect you to talk to dogs…I talked to them too…Those kinds of answers anger me. Now, boy, don't play foul with your father. Your mother was worried… I climbed a mountain, too…Where? What mountain? There are no mountains around here. What did you see? He smiled and did not answer. My anger caused me to hit him. My wife hit him! If he had smiled at you that way, you would have hit him too! He knew something. He wouldn't share it. What did he know? Then I would see him outside in the gravel pit talking to the children. He stood on top of the gravel heap and talked, talked and pointed. He gestured out over the city, through the streets and down toward the river. The children hanging on his every word, and some crying and some dancing and some laughing and all their eyes flying out over the city, following his words.

DON

My wife disciplines the children. She tells them if they continue in their naughtiness she will not smile at them.

AIME

And when I would come out the door to listen, he would stop. And he would give me that damned smile. After they told us he was gone, I took my wife into his room, and I put her down on his bed. She cried. She hasn't cried doing it since we were both in high school behind the gym. She usually laughs and sighs and throws herself up to me… I think she cried… A piece of plaster fell from the ceiling. It frightened us. We stopped. She asked me his name. I couldn't remember. She couldn't remember either. The doorbell rang. A huge crate was delivered. We opened it and found six dolls, life size, of him.

DON

That's right, you always get dolls to replace a loved one.

AIME

We placed them in a circle of chairs and asked each of him in turn his name. We even played scenes from his life, hoping it would remind us... Nothing. We sat there in the dark room on our chairs, silently, for two hours, trying to recall.

DON

We never sit in the room silently. Someone always says something.

AIME

He vanished for weeks at a time. That's why this time we paid it no mind. We didn't report it. We were used to it. He always returned. My wife always sent him to the market. He unleashed that smile on the butcher. The man grew so flustered he added an extra chop. He called later and told her never to send the boy again. He wouldn't serve him. But she did send him and each time after a more desperate phone call. Screaming, cursing, threatening the boy. The same with the shoemaker, the cleaner, the policeman... the old woman, the garbage man, the teacher, the gas man, the senator... They all called, screaming threats! He even went down to the river to watch the men in the torn overcoats drift along the promenade...

DON

He went down to watch the condemned? I didn't think you were supposed to watch them.

AIME

You're not. But he did. Always doing what he wanted. Not that he ever talked back to me. He just went out and did what he wanted and came back smiling and took his beating.

DON

What did he say about the condemned?

AIME

He said it was very cold at the river, so cold the men had to hunch over with their collars up. That's right. And whichever way they walked, they always faced into the wind. Yes... They never sat down, either. Always walking and watching the ice in the river...
(Closes his eyes to see his son describing it)
The ice passing out to sea... the men walking back and forth... Then something about salt crackers...

DON

Salt crackers? Oh, well–I believe that is what they feed those men.

AIME

Yes, he said the nuns stand behind the iron fence and throw the crackers down to them.

DON

From what I've heard, the gulls get most of it. They swoop in and snatch it right off the bricks. My wife knows a priest who told her about it.

AIME

Those are the people who committed blue light offenses, aren't they. That's why they watch the ice chunks float out to sea. They know they'll be flowing soon after. He said that when they are emaciated enough the wind pulls them right out of their shoes and carries them out to disappear under the cold water. Was he telling the truth? Vanished?

DON

According to the priest who got it from a nun who is allowed down there for the feedings, the promenade is strewn with old shoes. Piles of them here and there. Everywhere.

AIME

"And they never said a word" ...

DON

Oh, no, the condemned never speak. Silent as ghosts. Ha! Which
is what they become.

STEWARDESS' VOICE

If you will look out the windows on the right, ladies and
gentlemen, you will see below the Great Lakes of the North
American continent...

DON

Sounds like a nice trip.
   (Gets no response from AIME)
Yes, in rare instances planes go down, but gosh, you take a bigger
risk crossing the street. In any catastrophe that comes from the
air there is always one survivor. I would survive. I would. Did he
question our scene about that, too?
   (AIME nods)
That's very serious. My advice to you is to forget him completely.

AIME

I want to, but it's all so strange. I'm plagued with his damn
questions but I can't remember his name! You see, I must
disprove him, but to do it I have to get at that damn secret
knowledge he had. Now, if I could recall his name, it might lead
me to it. Isn't that true? If you know someone's name, it brings to
mind their face which in turn reminds you of their manner which
leads to gestures of their hands that point up the eyes. Once
you have their eyes you can drive down through them into the
place where they keep their secrets. Isn't that so? Then, when I
have the damn thing in my hand, I'll shake it till it shatters into a
thousand fraudulent pieces! And his questions will go shattering
with it! But how do I get at his name?

DON
(Growing anxious)
I... I don't know. It's not my field.

AIME
(Off on his own)
Henry... Harry...

DON
My uncle served in Taipei. He was chiropractor to the general staff. He said we'd hold it forever.

AIME
Lindon...

DON
After I surprise my wife, maybe I'll volunteer to serve over there. Probably win a medal.

YELLOW SIGNAL.

MUSIC STARTS.
(Jumping up)
DON
Yipes!
(Rushes over to the schedule chart)
The Housewife and the Postman!

(The TWO rush to the closet and furiously prepare as the room lights dim. DON puts on a woman's housecoat and wig. AIME puts on a postman's cap and takes out a letter. As the circle lights up, DON puts a chair in it and steps up on it)

AIME
(Studying the letter)
In here.
DON
What?

                              AIME

His name. Maybe it's in here.

                               DON

What?

              LIGHTS:THE RED SIGNAL flashes twice.

SOUND: A doorbell rings.
                               DON
                 (In a pleasantly womanish voice)
Who is it?
                              AIME
                 (Walks into circle; surly)
Postage due, seven cents.
                               DON

Bring it here, please.

                              AIME

You come down here, please.

                               DON

No–you bring it, please.

                              AIME

You want this letter or not?

                               DON

I can take it or leave it.

                              AIME

You just left it.
                 (HE exits the circle.DON waits.)

            SOUND:The doorbell rings again.

DON

Yes?

AIME
(Re-enters)
You gonna come down and take this letter?

DON

No.

AIME
I won't bring it up to you. It's not my job.
(DON smiles sweetly)
But it's a letter. It's from someone. Maybe it tells you they love
you and miss you. Or your brother was promoted or they are
sending you a painting from Italy... There might be money in it.
DON
I am expecting to hear that my sister gave birth. The country club
should notify us concerning our application. My husband's tax
refund is due also...

AIME
And you don't care? You're ready to let me walk out of here with
it? ... I don't walk up those stairs. If I do it for you I'll do it for
everyone . I don't get paid for that... I'll pay the seven cents.

DON

It's not the money.

AIME

Then what is it?

DON
I want complete service. No cheap meats or tattered shirts or
thirty dollar house calls that take the pulse and leave.

                              AIME
I won't bring it up.
                    (SHE outwaits him. HE climbs up on other chair)
Seven cents!

                    (The exchange is made. AIME storms out)

                              DON
Ta-daaaa!

                         LIGHTS:GREEN LIGHT:Flashes. Lights up
                         on room.

                    (DON removes his costume at closet. AIME takes
chairs back upstage and sits. He stares at the letter.)

DON
                    (As HE works)
The first thing, of course, is to get those panties off her. Some
ruse. Think up some innocent-seeming device.
                    (Looks up, sees AIME lost in his thoughts)
Did you hear what I said? Why are you standing there? Put the
letter away.

                              AIME
                    (To letter)
His name is in here.

                              DON
What?
                              AIME
They said we'd be notified. It must be my letter.

                              DON
Notified of the funeral.

AIME

They didn't say that. Just, "You'll be notified." They must have meant his name.

DON

How do you know they meant that?

AIME

How do you know they didn't?

DON

How do you know they did?

AIME

But they might have.

DON

But they might not!

AIME

But they might!

DON

Put it away.

(AIME puts the letter back in closet)

AIME
(Pacing the room)
Did you ever get a letter the way the scene says?

DON

Of course. My wife played the scene with a real postman only last week.

                              AIME
And did he deliver?

                              DON
They always deliver if you are polite but firm.

                              AIME
What did the letter look like?

                              DON
It had a lot of personal little scribbling, all over it.

                              AIME
And inside? Was there a name inside?

                              DON
I don't know. My wife reads the mail.
                    (AIME crosses to prop closet, takes out letter)
What are you doing? You're not thinking of opening it, are you?
You know what happened to the colored fellow in Studio 19?
After the green signal he opened the letter.

                              AIME
Did they give him a blue light?

                              DON
According to the janitor his whole body quivered when it flashed.

                              AIME
What happened to him?

                              DON
I don't know.

                              AIME
What was in the letter? A name?

                              DON

I don't know. Put it away.

                              AIME
                    (Puts letter away, but paces around prop closet
eyeing letter box)
Yes. Why not? It's quite possible the man in Studio 19 lost his son
and couldn't remember his name. After they told him he would
be notified he grew impatient. He couldn't wait for the postman
to deliver it, so he went ahead and opened it.

                              DON

My good feeling... It's drained out. Do you hear? I've got to think
of a way to get them off!
                              AIME
                    (Rushes to prop closet, takes out letter, reads
scribbling on back of envelope)
"Genoa is a big joke."

                              DON

Genoa is a big joke?

                              AIME

That's what is scrawled on the back.

                              DON

Genoa is in Italy.

                              AIME

The postmark is Cedar Rapids, Iowa.

                              DON

Is there a return address?

                              AIME

Klemper Garment Company

                          DON
Garments?

                          AIME
"418 Calle de la Revolucion."

                          DON
And the city?

                          AIME
No city, no country.

                          DON
Who is it addressed to?

                          AIME
Nobody.
              (Holds envelope up to light)
There is something in it. Writing.

                          DON
Writing? Maybe it's for me. Can you make out the word panties?

                          AIME
Too blurred. Can't make out anything.

                          DON
              (Takes letter)
Let me see.
              (Peers at letter, up to light)
Can't tell...
              (Hands letter back to AIME)

                          AIME
What if we...
              (Gestures opening letter)
But secretly. With our backs to them...

                            DON
Put it away!
                    (AIME puts letter back in cabinet)
Somebody's idea of a joke.

                            AIME
            (As THEY BOTH move around prop closet,
magnetized by letter)
No one is ever in here but us.
                    (Gestures to control booth)
Maybe him.

                            DON
He never comes in here. The janitor?

                            AIME
He can't write.

                            DON
Then you did it?

                            AIME
Maybe you.

                            DON
I don't make jokes.

                            AIME
Then it must have been me, though I don't remember.

                            DON
Childish thing to do.

                            AIME
I'm sorry.

DON

It is fine to say you are sorry after the damage is done. And I felt so good just a little while ago. You've drained it all out.

AIME

I won't do it again.

DON

Promise?

AIME

Forgive me?

DON

If you will do one thing.
                    (Glances furtively at control booth)
Tell me what you wrote in the letter.

AIME

I don't know what's inside!

DON

If that's the way you want to be...

AIME

I never looked inside. I only addressed it outside.

DON

Do you take me for a child? How do you know where to address it, if you don't know what 's in it? Your entire defense breaks down. You are not with me. You smile but you mean something else. You are planning retribution on me.

AIME

Retribution?

DON

Because you are jealous. For no good reason, since you play the housewife when we do the Negro version.

> (AIME smiles sheepishly, doubling DON's terror)

Ah, you see, hostile and aggressive!

AIME

I am confused.

DON

I am on to that one too. I is confused, Massa Don. I misses yo' meanin'. A pretty neat smoke screen to veil your trickery. You don't want me to surprise my wife, do you?

AIME

Yes, I mean, no, I mean...

DON

Why not? What is going on behind my back? She is always asking questions about you. Is he married? Does he dress well? She never asked about the others who were here with me. Why you? Do you know her?

AIME

Why, no.

DON

You've never seen her?

AIME

No, never.

DON

Do you swear it?

AIME

I swear!

                            DON
And you want me to surprise her?

                            AIME
Yes!

                            DON
And you believe I can?

                            AIME
Yes!

                            DON
Well, you better hope I do. Because if I don't succeed this time,
you're in trouble!
                 (Suddenly afraid of AIME's possible anger)
Are you angry? Don't be angry. Are we friends? Of course we are.
I will requisition another Negro version for you. Would you like
that? I will definitely put in for it. Say you're not angry.

                            AIME
I'm not angry.

                            DON
I believe you. I do.

             (AIME is drawn up to prop closet)

                            AIME
Do you think the postman will deliver to my home?

                            DON
Absolutely! If it has your boy's name, they'll deliver! Do you think
I'll succeed with my wife.
                            AIME
No question!

                            247

DON

But the panties. What about her goddam panties?

LIGHT:YELLOW SIGNAL.

MUSIC. Airplane Muzak type.

DON
(croses to chart)
Sole survivor. We better get ready.AIME, come on.

(AIME sets up two chairs in a circle. BOTH MEN put on their suit jackets and sit in chairs. THEY EACH have magazines)

AIME

Which is it? Oh, sole survivor. The white version?

DON

Yes, shhh...

AIME

What if she's in the laundry room? She might not hear him ring.

DON

Shhh, prepare.

AIME

Yes, let's see. It is a blue sky, serene, a yellow sun above and white clouds below. We glide along at forty thousand feet...
(THEY read in silence.)

LIGHTS:RED light flashes.

SOUND: The steady steady whistle of air for a long beat, then carrump.

                              AIME

What was that?

                              DON

I don't know. Look, the wing!
            (The Jets wind up into a scream. THEY plunge
downward.

                    LIGHT:Green and red lights whirl around
                    the circle.

                              DON

God! Help! God!

                              AIME

God.

                              DON

No! Nooooooo!

            BLACKOUT.

            SOUND:Silence. No sound of crash.

            LIGHTS:Circle lights come up again.

            (DON lies on the floor, his chair tipped over
            next to him. AIME lies crumpled beneath
            his chair.)

                              DON

We crashed.
            (DON looks around)
I am alive... I made it... I am alive!
            (Gets to his feet, winces)
Ow! My arm is broken.
            (Surveys the wreckage, then AIME)
All gone. Gee, he was with me just a moment ago.

                              249

CONTROLLER'S VOICE
(Over left speaker)
Closeup on body. Now back to Don. Good.

DON
Sitting next to me reading the financial section. Gee, I guess he did not have secret powers.
SOUND: sirens, trucks, helicopters.
Here come the rescuers. Won't they be surprised to find me alive.
(Sounds of MEN's VOICES amid the wreckage)
Here! Here I am!

MEN'S VOICES
There's someone in there! A survivor! There he is!

DON
And all I have is a broken arm!

ANNOUNCER'S VOICE
Are you all right?

DON
Are the reporters here and the TV and the radio and the movie people? Did they bring their cameras and recording apparatus?

ANNOUNCER'S VOICE
All right here.

DON
Oh, boy, great!

ANNOUNCER'S VOICE
How does it feel to be the sole survivor? Yes, right into the microphone.

DON

It feels great! I mean, this is a terrible tragedy. All these hundred fourteen people mangled up like this in the wreckage. It is a real shame , but I did have my secret powers,and that's what counts,isnt it? I'm sure everyone understands.

ANNOUNCER'S VOICE

Tell us how it happened.

DON

We were over the clouds and under the sun and the wing ripped off. You know how they do. And the plane went down in a scream.

ANNOUNCER'S VOICE

And what did you do?

DON

I cried out to God, of course, which is only human...

ANNOUNCER'S VOICE

Wonderful...

DON

Then, as the plane was going down, at the very moment it smashed into earth...

ANNOUNCER'S VOICE

Very moving description, smashed into earth. You did what?

DON

I jumped up.

ANNOUNCER'S VOICE

You jumped upward, thereby not crashing with the plane.

                                    DON

That is correct.

                         ANNOUNCER'S VOICE

Wonderful.

                                    DON

Except I broke my arm when I came down from jumping
upward. But I plan to continue perfecting this technique of crash
avoidance, so that in the future everyone with secret powers
will be able to come down from jumping up with no ill effects
whatever.

                         ANNOUNCER'S VOICE

Wonderful. And now, Sir, I wonder if you would demonstrate
your technique for viewers everywhere.

                                    DON

I'd be glad to. Are you ready?

                         ANNOUNCER'S VOICE

Ready whenever you are, Mr. Survivor.

                                    DON

Here it is!

                 (HE leaps up, as great white bulb flashes catch in
        mid-air.)

                               BLACKOUT

                  ROOM LIGHTS: Up on room.

                 (DON and AIME pace on opposite sides of the
        stage.
        AME comes down front and addresses the control booth)

AIME

What if she's in the bathroom? Hello? Hello? Tell them to keep ringing.

DON

(To himself)

If I close all the windows, so the room gets good and stuffy, then it would be quite natural for her to take them off.

CURTAIN

END OF ACT I

ACT II
SCENE I

DON and JANE's apartment. Early the same evening. The living room is modern. Up right is a desk. Down center a modern sofa. On either side of it are two Danish modern chairs. A door up left leads off to the hall and kitchen. There are no windows, no paintings. The room is barren of decorations, yet sleek and expensive.

AT RISE: (DON and JANE sit in the Danish chairs, facing out front, watching a program on a wall-size TV set. THEY are bathed in a grey light. From the set come the sounds of two mating cats. The scene is punctuated by their cries. JANE is dressed in sweater, skirt and heels.)

JANE

He is moving toward her.
(Leans forward in her chair)
He is beside her.

DON

It is very warm in here.
(Waits for a response–None comes)
I feel overdressed. Do you feel overdressed?
(No response)
Our entire society is overdressed. We are smothering in cloth.
(SHE ignores him)
It is sapping our national health, if you ask me.

JANE

Shhhh. Watch the program!

DON

(After a moment of silence)
Mind you, I'm not talking about top clothes. We need them to
protect our pores from infection. I am talking about underwear.
It is nothing but a hangover from the days before central heating.
You agree, Jane?
(No response)
You take underpants, for example. Panties are nothing more
than a cultural lag. Back in feudal society they served a function.
Those castles were cold. Not only that, sexuality was taboo and
considered the work of the Devil. But today, to be the slaves
of an outworn creed that orders us to wear underpants! It is an
injustice! If it were up to me I would rip off everybody's under
pants right where they stand! Free them of their chattels! Jane,
you agree?

JANE

Don, you are not watching.

DON

Yes, I am. These cats take forever before they do anything. Did
you hear what I said?

JANE

We'll talk about it afterward, dear. Now, watch your program.
(They watch)
Oh!

DON

Cats don't wear underpants.

JANE

Oh!

DON

Need to return to nature.
            (Despite himself is drawn to action on the screen)
Good boy! He's licking her ear.

JANE

She's permitting him to lick her ear.

DON

Yes, but he's doing it.

JANE

Only because she lets him.

DON

She's rolling over on her back.

JANE

Let him try something in that position.

DON

That's true. Cats are constructed differently.
            (Jumps slightly)
He's pawing her belly!
            (His hand to his left eye)
Oh!
                                        JANE
She clawed his eye! She clawed him!

DON

Ooh, look at him slink away. Poor beggar, is he seriously hurt?

JANE

The blood is running down his cheek.
            (Sees DON feeling his eye)
Oh, Don, stop it. He's not hurt badly. You take it so personally, as
if it was real.

DON

Aren't we supposed to take it that way?

JANE

Yes, but there is no need to get so involved. You've seen this program a dozen times. You know that he's not really hurt, merely rebuffed.
(DON drops his hand)
That's the way it should be, isn't it?
(HE nods)
Why?

DON

So he'll be grateful when she lets him.

JANE

She's careful not to hurt him seriously.
(DON nods)
Why?

DON

If he were seriously injured, he could'nt perform.

JANE

You see, you know all the right answers. Now, aren't your fears dispelled?
(DON nods, but turns away from the set, fingering his eye)
Sometimes I don't understand you. You never react this way to the dog program. They aren't exactly gentle about it. The lady dog nips the boy dog's heels constantly.

DON

She's playful.

JANE

She is not playful, I assure you.

                           DON

She never draws blood.

                           JANE

That doesn't mean she's playful. She has pity on him. Too much, if
you ask me.
               (After a moment)
Donald, you turn around this very minute and watch.
               (HE hesitates)
How will you write your report if you don't watch? You know
what they told you. If this report isn't more detailed than last
week's they will have serious reservations about scheduling
anything for us next week. Have you forgotten what they
promised for us next week?

                           DON

Horses.

                           JANE

Two Japanese beach horses. Remember how thrilling they were
last year? How they whinnied and rose up, their hoofs beating
the air? How she galloped away again and again?

                           DON

And how he finally cornered her in the corner between the fence
posts?

                           JANE

She cried out in pain.

                           DON

Did she? I thought she enjoyed it.

                           JANE

Don't you remember? That's what you said in your report and
they marked you wrong...

JANE(CONT'D)
(HE nods)
Don't you want the horses back?
(Meaningfully)
I do.
(HE nods)
Then do as I say.

DON

Isn't it warm in here? I'm very warm. I think I'll take off my underpants.

JANE

Take off your what?

DON

(Points to the screen)
It makes me sweat.

JANE

It is supposed to, dear.

DON

Does it make you sweat?

JANE

A little.

DON

Why don't you take yours off, too? No sense being uncomfortable.

JANE

I'm not uncomfortable.

DON

You said you were sweating.

JANE

A little sweat is a sweet reminder of things past.

DON

We sweated very little.

JANE

Enough, dear. Enough for me.
                    (Movement on the screen)
Oh... Oh...

DON

He is creeping up on her...

JANE

He is coming up from behind...

DON
                    (Fingering his eye)
He is going to surprise her.

JANE

She has her back to him.

DON

Shhh! ... A few inches more... Oh!
                    (Grabs his other eye)

JANE

Bravo! She clawed the other eye!
                    (To cat on screen)
Naughty boy, that's what you get.
                    (SHE sits back, then)
Oh!
DON
                    (Jumps up)
He's got her! Bleeding from both eyes, but he's got her!

JANE
(Jumping up)
His teeth in her nape!

DON
Beautiful!

JANE
Don't let him!

DON
Yes, yes!

JANE
Noooo!

DON
He's there! There!

JANE
Damn him!

(A silence follows for a few moments as BOTH nod
   their heads in tempo to the rhythm of the act on
   the screen. THEY grow more rigid as THEY do.
Quickly, tell me who I am.

DON
The queen...

JANE
The queen of what?

DON
Queen of the African Plains.

                        JANE

Yes, describe me.

                        DON

You wear a black leopard skin...

                        JANE

Not my dress, idiot, my body!

                        DON

You... your legs are two white panthers, sleek and stalking. Your thighs are a lioness waiting all aquiver in the high grass.

                        JANE

Yes! For who?

                        DON

Your lover...

                        JANE

Name him! Name him!

                        DON

The African Lion!

                        JANE

The Black Lion!

                        DON

Black...

                        JANE

My breasts? ...

                        DON

Breasts? ... Uh... er...

                                JANE

Hurry!

                                DON

Your breasts are... I forget.

                                JANE

Two–pink...

                                DON

Two pink pussy cats... Do I have to go on?

                                JANE

Two pink pussy cats waiting to be devoured!
        (Briefly turns away from the screen to give him a
venomous, demanding look)
My eyes!

                                DON

Are those of a maddened jaguar.

                                JANE

Burning!

                                DON

Burning with hunger and...

                                JANE

Hate!

                                DON

Hate!

                                JANE

Hunger and hate! Hunger and hate! And then? ...

                    DON

The Lion lopes...

                    JANE

The Black Lion, fool!

                    DON

The Black-as-the-ace-of-spades-Lion lopes into the clearing.
            (Rapidly, staccato)
Aloof, as if he doesn't see you, but he does, and his eyes are cool,
cool, but smoldering, smoldering, he approaches, making throaty
sounds. Arggghhh–you warn him off...!

                    JANE
            (Viciously)
Arghh!

                    DON

But he leaps!

                    JANE

Arggghhh!

                    DON

His black paws on your pink pussy-cats. His black loins on your
blond lioness! His black flanks pressing your white panthers. You
claw his eyes!

                    JANE

Arrgghh!

                    DON

But he presses!
            (In rhythm)
Press-Press-Press-Press-Press...!

TV CATS
(From out front, in a mutual wail)

Arrgghhh!

JANE
(Screaming)

Arrgghhh!

DON
(Weakly imitates)

Argh!

JANE
(Falls back into chair)

Ahhhh.

DON
(Pretends to fall back into his)

Did you?

JANE

Of course, don't I always?

DON

Yes, with them.

JANE

Why are you so hostile? Didn't you?

DON
(Hesitates)

Yes... I did, shhh.

JANE

You did not. I can tell. You hesitated in answering.

DON

No, please, I did.
      (In a whisper)
Not so loud. We might be heard.

JANE

      (Whispering)
Don't lie to me!

DON

But I did! a little.

JANE

But not enough! Why didn't you? You never do!

DON

I'm sorry...

JANE

Sorry. You leave me alone, then you're sorry. The damage is done.

DON

Maybe I don't because you have me describing everything.

JANE

That's right. Project your inadequacies on to me.

DON

No, no, I'm not blaming you. You are a warm and loving woman.

JANE

You are jealous, because I am the one who hands in the reports to them.

DON

No, not at all. I respect you for that. I admire you. You are a wonderful person, a witty companion, a generous mother, staunch friend, and… and…

JANE

….Very patriotic.

DON

Very. Don't be annoyed. I'll do it next time. I promise.

JANE

Next time is all very well, but what are you going to put on your report for this time?

DON

I 'll say I did.

JANE

How will you describe it, if you didn't?

DON

Describe yours to me, and I'll…

JANE

Oh, darling, you know that's not allowed. Besides, they'll know it's mine. They know me. They know you.

DON
(Rises, paces–in a frustrated whisper)
They know everything!
(Stops, looks around, listens)

JANE
(Cool)
Be careful.

DON
(Goes to her)
Maybe I could remember last time. Last week was... Let's see,
foxes?

JANE
You see, you can't even remember what they were.

DON
Squirrels? A small animal, I know. I kept losing them behind the
radish sprouts. Minks?

JANE
Marmots. You have no memory at all. We'll never get the horses.
(HE paces again)
This might even affect things at the studio.

DON
What do you mean?

JANE
You said yourself that colored fellow is trying to push you out.

DON
Out to destroy me!

JANE
If your prestige falls too low in their eyes...

DON
Something might happen to me! What?

JANE
I don't know.

DON

A blue light? Would they? For nothing? I haven't done a thing!
I never do anything. That is how I have survived, by not doing
anything! Now, for no reason they are going to do something! They
can't! They can't listen to him! He's unreliable! He's aggressive!
He's...Black! Oh, my gosh, first the room, then the river, then...
(Shivers)
I'm cold. Oh, I'm so cold!

JANE

(Puts her arm around his shoulder)
There, there. No one will do anything to you. You leave it to me,
dear. I'll think up something for you.

DON

(Falls to his knees, embraces her legs)
Oh, thank you, thank you!

JANE

Yes. Get up, dear, you'll catch cold in your knees.
(HE rises–SHE points to the TV set)
Now, I'll get to work.

(HE rises.. SHE crosses and sits at desk, takes out
paper and pen and starts writing.
HE sits down on sofa.A silence ensues. JANE slumps wearily in
her chair)

DON

What's the matter?

JANE

I'm tired.

DON

Do you want to rest awhile?

JANE

Not tired that way. These days I grow suddenly weary, as if I was carrying a great stone without feeling its weight, until suddenly I crumple.

DON

You should see a doctor.

JANE

Do you remember when we were in high school, the dance at the Riverside Country Club?

DON

When we used to hang out with the Mexican kids?

JANE

All the boys were in blue suits. The girls wore white gowns. Mexican girls are beautiful in white.

DON

The boys were given white gardenias at the door.

JANE

And we wore white gardenias.

DON

Yes, the room was thick with sweat and gardenias.

JANE

We danced La Bamba again and again all night long.

DON

I was drinking beer and vodka.

JANE

Mr. Hutchins caught you.

DON

I was wild then; I didn't care.

JANE

Remember Chuey D'Arcy? How he jumped up on the banquet table and started to sing?

DON

He was wild then; he didn't care.

JANE

And then you jumped up there with him. The two of you singing and dancing.

DON

We were wild then; we didn't care.

JANE

And the rest of us screaming, "Go!-Go!-Go!"...

DON

And chairs flying! ...

JANE

Go!-Go!-Go! ...

DON

And teachers running! ...

JANE

Go!-Go!-Go! ...

DON

And then the green uniforms! ...

JANE

Go!-Go!-Go! ...

DON

And then the shot!
       (Silence)
And Chuey fell to the floor.

(THEY BOTH regard the dead body on the floor)

JANE

And at the funeral the next day...

DON

No, that's enough.

JANE

Remember Paul Sanchez?

DON

I don't want to.

JANE

Please, Don...

DON

I don't like that memory.

JANE

Please, it helps overcome my weariness... Remember Mickey
Rollins?

DON
(Reluctantly)
He was there.

JANE
And Paul Santana?...who else?

DON
Joel Golden...

JANE
And Helen Dudick and Isabel Ramon and I. Go on. We come out of
Immaculate Heart Church into the bright sun...

DON
Angry. Young faces angry in the June sun.
(HE rises, comes forward)
Justice. Justice for the martyred boy! The procession down the
street.

(SHE rises, BOTH face front, marking time with
their feet)

JANE
Hundreds walking his casket down Soto Street...

DON
Then the green uniforms ahead...

JANE and DON
Mur-ders! Mur-der-ers! ...

DON
Then...
(Cries out)
Tear gas! Fire in my eyes!

                    JANE
You kept on!

                    DON
Fire in my mouth!

                    JANE
You marched!

                    DON
Fire in my throat!

                    JANE
Bravely!

                    DON
Shots! Run!
            (THEY break rank, scatter)

                    JANE
The casket, don't drop it!

                    DON
Run, Raul! Get up!

                    JANE
            (As Raul)
My face! Don, my face is bleeding!

                    DON
Oh, Jesus, you're hit!
            (Starts to cross to her, is hit in leg)
Aiee!
            (SHE drops to one knee)
My leg!
            (HE crawls)

JANE

The casket! They dropped the casket!
                    (SHE clutches her stomach)
I'm sick!

DON
                    (Calling out to other young people)
Scattered! The young people scattered! The casket alone! Oh,
Chuey, we left you alone!

JANE
                    (Reaches out to him on floor)
But you fought!

DON

We thought we could win!

JANE

You were a man!

DON

Winners are men, losers are dogs!

JANE

I loved you then! I wanted to give you everything!

                    (This last outcry brings silence. They BOTH see
                    where THEY are on the floor. DON rises to
                    his feet, turns away from her. The silence is
                    embarrassed)

DON

It was stupid to march! We surprised them. We frightened them
with our numbers and our angry faces. When you frighten them,
they react violently. We should have sent a delegation to reason
with them. A few... a few calm, calm, reasonable young people.
After all, they did have the power...

JANE
(Studying him, as if seeing him truly for the first time)
We were married soon after.

DON
Now we are with them.

JANE
(Sadly)
We are winners.

DON
It's better here with them. Not to boast, but I'm in a very responsible position. They don't hand out jobs like mine to just anyone. I earned it. They respect me. More than that I really think they like me. What I mean is they have a personal feeling for me. I can sense it. Sometimes a memo comes out of the schedule machine with a little joke on it. A witty saying or clever remark. Not handwritten mind you. Their machine won't process handwriting, faxed, but still a personal little witticism. They wouldn't do that with just anyone. That's the kind of thing you do with a friend. Don't you think?

JANE
(Turned away from him)
We've gone too far.

DON
Don't you think, Jane?

JANE
Yes, dear, I do think so.
(Briskly as SHE crosses back to desk)
Now, let's get back to our little joke.

DON
What joke? What are you talking about?

JANE

Nothing, dear, I was making a witticism like your friends at work. Now I had best do these reports. You relax and do whatever you wish.

(SHE resumes her task, writes. HE sits on the sofa)

DON

What a wonderful woman. I'm a lucky man. I found a gem in the desert of life. How could I ever think of wanting to surprise her? I know how much being surprised upsets her, yet I persist, willfully, maliciously. There is no question; I have sadistic tendencies!

JANE

Are you mumbling, dear? I asked you not to mumble in the living room. Did you forget?

DON

Sorry.

JANE
(Not looking up from her work)
If you want to mumble, go in the john.
(JANE pulls at her dress)
That is the proper place for it, where you won't disturb others.

DON

I won't mumble, dear.
(SHE pulls at her dress again)
What's the matter?

JANE

I have a chafing on my inner leg.

DON

A chafing?

JANE

Yes, my under-garments have irritated it.

DON

Your under-garments?

JANE

(Rises)

I think I had better take them off.

(SHE stands behind sofa and removes her underpants)

DON

(To himself)

Is it possible? No, I can't! She just saved my life!

JANE

That's better. Let the air get at it. Air is a natural healer. My skin is so tender. White people generally have tender skin.

(Sits back at desk)

Colored people have leathery skin. I'm not surprised after thousands of years slaving in the sun. They all have bunchy muscles and crude, tough skin.

(Starts writing)

Darling, does that colored fellow have a muscular body?

DON

(To himself)

There she goes again. More questions about him. Is he married? Does he speak well? Black lions and black men!

JANE

(Looks up)

Did you hear me, dear?

DON

No, he's... average.

JANE

Are you all right?

DON

Fine, fine.

JANE

That colored fellow hasn't got you frightened, has he?

DON

No, no.

JANE

You haven't promised to requisition new scenes for him, have you? Out of fear?
(HE shakes his head no)
Now, tell me why you shouldn't.

DON

To act out of fear is to relinquish authority...

JANE

And? ...

DON

And only encourages rebellion.

JANE

That's right. We mustn't be generous out of fear. They count on that. That's why they sulk so much. Even when they smile, you know it's only to terrify you. What kind of hands does he have, dear? Are they big as hams? The kind that could maul you?

DON

Average hands, average.

JANE

Then there's nothing to be afraid of, is there? You occupy
yourself, dear, while I do this...
                    (In a whisper)
For both of us.
                    (Blows him a kiss. HE smiles weakly. SHE turns
back to her work)

DON

                    (To himself)
That does it. She's wild for him. Well, my dear, gratitude is dead.
Prepare yourself for a surprise.
                    (To her)
Aren't you hungry?

JANE

Hungry? We had dinner only two hours ago.

DON

Still, I feel like a snack.

JANE

What would you like?

DON

Pot roast

JANE

Don't be ridiculous.

DON

Why don't we have a pot roast party? A late dinner party. I'll go
wake up the kids. They might want to play in the living room.

JANE

Wake them up? I only just put them down.

DON

Just for a while.

JANE

Don't be silly, dear, they need their rest. If you want a sandwich, go in the kitchen. There's some cold salami in the ice box.

DON

Cold salami? But it's so cold.

JANE

Well, heat it up in the oven.

DON

Good idea. Would you do it for me...dear?

JANE

I would, but you see how much I have to do.

DON

It won't take long.

JANE

To heat your salami?

DON

You don't have to heat it all the way. Just bend over and put it in.

JANE

And who will keep an eye on it to see it doesn't burn?

DON

I will, gladly.

JANE

If you have time to watch it, dear, then you have time to bend
over and put it in yourself. Go on, now, if you want to heat it up,
you do it without me.

DON

You won't even help me with it?

JANE

You call me when you are ready, and I'll come and take it out for
you. Go ahead.

      (HE exits. SHE turns back to the desk and resumes
writing.

SOUND: An ice box opening and closing offstage.

      (DON appears in the doorway holding an enormous
salami in his two hands. He sneaks up behind her. She crumples a
piece of paper and throws it at the waste basket under the desk.
It misses. She stands and bends over to pick it off the floor. DON
rushes toward her with the salami. SHE straightens up at the last
moment and turns to face him.Innocently)

JANE

What are you doing?

DON

(Helpless, exposed, crude, etc.)
Is...Is...Is this the...the salami you meant...dear?

JANE

Of course, it is, dear. Can't you tell a salami when you see one?
      (Starts to sit, stops)
I was just thinking. It is silly to stick the whole thing in the oven. Why
don't you slice off a few pieces and fry them? Are you all right, dear?

      (HE nods weakly)
Good, you do that then.

DON

(HE doesn't move. HE has collapsed inside himself)
Jane... Am I alright?

JANE

You're fine, dear.

DON

And... is everything all right? I mean, if a catastrophe came from
the air, I would survive, wouldn't I?
(SHE nods)
The postman always delivers...

JANE

Up the stairs...

DON

And we will hold Taipei...

JANE

Forever.

DON

Forever. Why will we? I forgot why.

JANE

We have the air power. The sea power...

DON

...sea power...

JANE

Stand up straight, dear. Be affirmative.

DON

The sea power...

                    JANE
Full voice.

                    DON
The sea power!

                    JANE
Louder!

                    DON
I can't!

                    JANE
Sing!

                    DON
Oh beautiful for spacious skies...

                    JANE
Bigger!

                    DON
For amber waves of grain...

                    TV VOICES
There's no doubt, doctor, we will have to operate...

                    JANE
More!

                    DON
America, America...

                    TV VOICES
But the risk, doctor, think of the risk...

JANE

Sing!

(SHE begins to laugh)

DON

Jane, please! God shed his grace on thee...

TV VOICES

We have no choice, doctor...

DON

And crown thy good with brotherhood; from sea to shining sea...

BLACKOUT.

IN BLACKOUT.

2ND DOCTOR VOICE

But, doctor, this patient is Italian.

1ST DOCTOR VOICE

We will just have to improvise.

2ND DOCTOR VOICE

But, doctor, a tracheal dichotomy?

1ST DOCTOR VOICE

The fate of the entire surrealist movement depends on this man.

2ND DOCTOR VOICE

But, doctor, we are veterinarians.

1ST DOCTOR VOICE

I don't care what kind of Aryans we are. The patient comes first.

2ND DOCTOR VOICE

But, doctor, we treat only animals.

1ST DOCTOR VOICE

That's all right, this man is a horse.

2ND DOCTOR VOICE

Yes, doctor, but a sea-horse.

1ST DOCTORVOICE

You have a good eye for details.

2ND DOCTOR VOICE

But, doctor...

1ST DOCTOR VOICE

Hush, you wonderful man. Call me a cab.

2ND DOCTOR VOICE

But, doctor...

1ST DOCTOR VOICE

And stop calling me doctor, I'm your sister.

2ND DOCTOR VOICE

But, sis...

1ST DOCTOR VOICE

If you're good, next semester, I will teach you the violin. Now kiss me goodbye, the Indians are attacking.

2ND DOCTOR VOICE

Which are you, my sister or my doctor?

1ST DOCTOR VOICE

I'm your sissy doctor.

LIGHTS UP ON:

ACT II
SCENE II

       Time the same. AIME's apartment. It is a cavernous room, bare walled and rundown. There is a table and many chairs.

     (AIME sits watching the screen downstage. HE is thinking. VIOLA dances slowly on the other side of the stage to a blues.

MUSIC: "Green Onions" by Booker T.

AIME

Are you sure the postman didn't come?
       (Pause)
Will you turn that off? I am trying to think.

VIOLA

It comforts me to dance.

AIME

You know how they feel about that kind of music.

VIOLA

They can't hear it. It's too low. Besides, I want to enjoy myself.

AIME

You'll never be civilized.

VIOLA

     (teasing)
Savage.

VIOLA(CONT'D)
(HE turns away)
Aren't you going to bite my nose?
(HE ignores her)
Or pull my fingers?
(SHE laughs)

AIME

I had to tell him something. He stood over me. It is hard to know his mind. Sometimes he wants me Negro, other times white.

VIOLA

Today he wanted you Negro.

AIME

Most of the day, yes.

VIOLA

(Sings as SHE dances)
"I got a savage,
Other side of town." .... .
(HE jumps up, turns off music)
If I don't dance, I cry. You want me to cry?

AIME

I want you to help me. You were the one who started it. When the plaster fell, you asked his name. You wanted to know.

VIOLA

I only wanted to know then, while you were holding me.

AIME

And after, when we sat in the circle with the dolls.

VIOLA

Can't you just enjoy yourself, and let it be forgotten? We can have other children.

AIME

Not like him.

VIOLA

You can never let anything rest.

AIME

He had a secret. He knew something, something that would open the world, answer all the questions. Why shouldn't I want to know it?

VIOLA

They don't want you to know.

AIME

What do you mean? Did they call? Were you warned?

VIOLA

You were so sweet this morning after they told us. You carried me to bed, shouting and weeping. You gave me your pain the way you used to when we lived on Washington Avenue.

AIME

Viola, were you warned?

VIOLA

A man's pain turns to sweetness inside a woman.

AIME

Did they warn you not to think about him?

VIOLA

Can I have your sweetness again? Tonight?

AIME

Answer me.

VIOLA

(Sharply)
If I can't have that, I want my music.

AIME

I want to know.

VIOLA

(Sings)
"I want to know,
I want to know,
I want to…"
(HE grabs her)
The postman came today.

AIME

He did? Why didn't you tell me? Where is the letter? Did you open it? Where is it?

VIOLA

Wait! I did what you told me. I was polite but firm. When he left the first time I waited at the head of the stairs.

AIME

Just as the scene says, good. Then when he returned…?

VIOLA

He never returned.

AIME

What?

VIOLA

I stood at the head of the stairs for three hours. I didn't move a muscle. He never came back.

AIME

That is impossible.

VIOLA

At four o'clock I went to the kitchen for bread and an apple.

AIME

That's when he returned! You missed him!

VIOLA

I was only gone a minute. Besides, I would have heard the bell tinkle over the door. I came right back. I waited three more hours till the stairs grew dark.

AIME

And he never...?

VIOLA

The door was still. If they wanted you to know they would have had him deliver it.

AIME

But if they didn't want me to know, they'd send me a blank memo or a phone call with silent breathing on the other end. That's how they do it. You must have done something wrong. You must follow the scene exactly.

VIOLA

I did!

AIME

You didn't! I know you! When you don't care enough about something, you do it sloppily.

VIOLA

I was letter perfect.

AIME

Then he would have delivered. Don's wife tried it last week. No problem. Up the stairs, seven cents, ta-daaa! What did you say?

VIOLA

We both said the words of the scene until I said, firmly but not too firmly and politely, very politely, "I can take it or leave it."

AIME

And he said, "You just left it."

VIOLA

He said, "I am not walking up any flight of stairs for any black madonna." Then he turned and he shut the door behind him.

AIME

Black Madonna? That's not in either version. He must have been drunk. A sober man wouldn't say black madonna. Did he stagger when he said it?
(SHE shakes her head negatively)
Was his tongue thick? He sloshed his words.
(SHE shakes her head, again)
Bring out the dolls.

VIOLA

You tried those damn dolls five times already.

AIME

They have his name. Get them.

VIOLA

Will you pick me up and carry me into the bedroom later?

AIME

Black Madonna
        (SHE exits)
Could be a frustrated artist. They think of madonnas constantly.

        (SHE returns with a three-year-old Negro doll in a
snow suit)

AIME

This time we won't wait till the end of the memory. If a name
comes to you, say it. Viola, are you listening?

VIOLA

Aren't you afraid they might catch you using them wrong?

AIME

What do you mean wrong? They sent the dolls to replace him…

VIOLA

To play with the way you play with ordinary children.

AIME

No one said how I should use them.

VIOLA

You never let the truth get in your way, do you? You go right on
believing what you want.

AIME

Be careful, woman.

VIOLA

I pity you the day you wake up.

AIME

Begin!

VIOLA

Oh, so-and-so, you have snow all over you.

AIME

Stop. Can't you say a name instead of so-and-so?

VIOLA

Oh. Victor, you have snow...

AIME

Victor! You're teasing me. You know I would never christen my child Victor. I am Negro.

VIOLA

A savage one.

AIME

Begin again.

VIOLA

Oh, Roosevelt, You have snow all over you.

AIME
(In baby voice)
I built a snowman. It was pushed over.

VIOLA

Someone pushed it over? Who?

AIME

I don't know.

VIOLA

Was it a passerby?

                    AIME

The street was empty.

                    VIOLA

Then it was the wind.

                    AIME

Georgie! Then it was the wind, Georgie!

                    VIOLA

Georgie?

                    AIME

George.

                    VIOLA

Then it was the wind, Georgie.
          (THEY BOTH shake their heads, resume)
Then it was the wind.
                    AIME
          (As child)
There was no wind.

                    VIOLA

You didn't build it strong enough.

                    AIME

I built it thick with a small head.

                    VIOLA

          (Takes doll in her lap)
Then it has happened to you. This is your first lesson. As you go
through life bad things will happen to you. You will never know
who did it or why. And Momma won't know and Daddy won't
know...

AIME
(As himself, takes doll)
At such times you must accept what has happened and begin all over again.

VIOLA
(As child)
I know what pushed it over.

AIME
You do? Tell us.

(The doll is silent)

Even then he knew and wouldn't answer. Tell us, Albert.

VIOLA
Tell us, Samuel.

AIME
William, tell us.

VIOLA
Lawrence, if you tell us, I'll give you a dish of ice cream. I'll even pour a little coffee on it, the way you like it.

AIME
(Pacing now)
Maybe he was a new man, not familiar with the scene.

VIOLA
He was letter perfect.

AIME
Bring the next...Black Madonna... Black Madonna...

(SHE brings in a five-year-old doll)

VIOLA

(As child)
What is factory grease?

AIME

We don't have it anymore, William.

VIOLA

Is it good?

AIME

It dirties your hands, Alvin.

VIOLA

Are dirty hands bad?

AIME

Clean hands are better.

VIOLA

Can clean hands be dirty?

AIME

What do you mean? What do you mean? Answer me, boy.

VIOLA

(As herself)
That's all he said.

AIME

Criticizing me, his eyes were always criticizing me.
(To the boy)
It was senseless over on Washington Avenue. Senseless in the
factory. Daytimes I was the arm of a machine. Nighttimes a black
face under the street lights. I wanted to be a man.'

VIOLA

Leave him be. He won't answer.

AIME

Never answered. Only that smile.
(To the doll)
You were too young. You don't remember the night the rat crept into your crib. You've forgotten how you screamed when he bit you. You children have short memories. Did you want to grow up screaming? Did you?
(VIOLA has brought in a six-year-old doll. AIME takes it, continues his address to it)
Animals bite animals. That is the law of their kingdom, But when a rat bites a child, where is the sense? You are being treated like an animal, no different from the lice on your head. You pluck a louse and squeeze it till the blood pops out. The life of a bug means nothing. It was born hungry and died full. No more to say. It thought nothing, built nothing. It was nothing and need not have lived at all. Did you want that for us? We lived in dirt. It covered the walls, the chairs, the blankets. Even the light bulb hanging in the middle of the room was grimy so it gave off a dirty glow. Dirt is for animals.

VIOLA

(As child)
Do we have neighbors?

AIME

I'm not finished! We will have this out once and for all! I'm sick of his constant carping, his superior smile! He never forgave me for bringing us here. He would rather we stayed in our hole on Washington Avenue to listen to people like Sammy Roach jamming a knife into his mother, then his father, then his sisters and baby brothers.
(To doll)

AIME(CONT'D)

You have conveniently blotted that from your child's brain. I know your tricks. And at the police station, when they asked him why he did it, he said he didn't know. And when his aunt asked him in his cell, and she cupped his hands gently in hers, he still didn't know. And when they walked him up the last steps, even then he didn't know. Animals do not know. Their last day is as blind as their first.

VIOLA

(As child)
What happens to you when you get a blue light?

AIME

What? He never asked that! Why did you ask that?

VIOLA

I don't know.

AIME

You too! You blame me too! Because I took you away from your Saturday night dances! All those black legs writhing and kicking under the red lights! The shrieking laughter of the fat women in the corner! You loved it! But it was angry laughter, laughter at white ladies, at THEM! Laughter that led to trouble. To Polack boys trapping me in an alley! To Irish boys spreading you apart in a vacant lot! To Italian boys stuffing Lou Jones in a water barrel! Trouble! Trouble! Blindness and trouble! Meaningless murder, and you loved it!

VIOLA

Aime, no...

AIME

You have sabotaged me ever since! You sent the postman away!

VIOLA

No!

AIME

Lies! I am surrounded by lies!
>(Stops, catches himself)
What is happening to me?
>(THEY sit in silence)
Bring the next.
>(SHE exits)
He will return. He always does. There's nothing in the scene that says it has to be right then. No time limit. That can't be. It might be years. He might return after we are gone. Doesn't make sense.
>(HE thinks. VIOLA returns with seven-year-old doll)
The letter wasn't for us. It was for a neighbor. He was in the door before he realized his mistake. In order to escape he said what he did. Describe the letter.

VIOLA

It was thick and bulky. Postmarks all over it and lots of stamps. It was covered with scribblings.

AIME

Could you make them out?

VIOLA

Only one. When he held the letter up to taunt me, I could see it.

AIME

What did it say?

VIOLA

"Genoa is a big joke."

>(A pause...then AIME takes the doll, nods for her to begin. SHE stands silent)

AIME

Start.

VIOLA

I don't want to remember him. I want to make another child to take his place. I'm still young enough and it's what I know how to do. I don't understand what you are after.

AIME

I'm after the thing that gives ... the ... meaning ... .

VIOLA

That's why you brought us here?

AIME

Their life makes sense. They have answers for questions.

VIOLA

Then why plague the boy?

AIME

He knew something.

VIOLA

What?

AIME

I don't know. Begin.

VIOLA

(As child)
Do we have neighbors?

AIME

Of course, downstairs and to either side.

                    VIOLA
Did you ever see them?

                    AIME
We never have.

                    VIOLA
Did you knock on their door?

                    AIME
When we moved in, yes.

                    VIOLA
What happened?

                    AIME
There was no answer.

                    VIOLA
Did they knock on our door?

                    AIME
The following day.

                    VIOLA
What happened?

                    AIME
We didn't answer.

                    VIOLA
Why not?

                    AIME
We didn't know who it was. It might have been anyone.

VIOLA

Did you hear their voices?

AIME

The woman said, "No one lives here." The man asked, "Then who knocked on our door?" She answered, "I don't know. Come. It's cold in the hallway." And they left.

VIOLA

I knocked on the door upstairs today
                    (As herself)
What happened?
                    (As child)
A little girl with white hair opened the door. She said she was lonely in the afternoon.
                    (As herself)
You didn't go inside, did you?
                    (As child)
She gave me coffee and a sandwich on the sofa.
                    (A pause, then VIOLA as herself)
Aime, it's your line.

AIME

What?

VIOLA

You have to say, "What did you talk about?"

AIME

He must have come straight from church where they ridiculed him into an exorbitant offering. Naturally he was resentful and needed to punish someone. So he called you black madonna and left.

VIOLA

You didn't try one name this whole last scene.

                              AIME

Tomorrow he'll feel better. He'll see his duty and return.
                    (AIME is up and pacing. VIOLA turns on her music
and resumes dancing)

MUSIC:"Dock Of The Bay", Otis Redding.

                              AIME

He's really a very nice fellow. It was silly of me to be angry at him.
Any man can have a bad day. It's what makes us human. Tomorrow,
he'll play the scene as it should be. Just to make sure, though, I
want you to bake him a chocolate cake. You're not listening.

                              VIOLA

The scene has no chocolate cake.

                              AIME

There's nothing in it that says you couldn't be holding a chocolate
cake in your hands.
                              VIOLA
What if he don't like chocolate cake?

                              AIME

Doesn't, not don't. Everybody likes chocolate.

                              VIOLA

Some people doesn't. It reminds them of us.

                              AIME

Don't, not doesn't. Bake him a white cake, too, with white icing.
You can hold one in each hand. Then he can choose.

                              VIOLA

A white cake might be bad, too, remind him of himself.

AIME

Are you making fun of me? I'm serious.

VIOLA

I doesn't don't make no fun of you, Mistuh Aime.

AIME

That is not very funny.

VIOLA

Savage. Why don't I bake him a blue cake on my right foot and a yellow on my left, and on my elbows a green and red cake and on my head the biggest blackest cake you ever saw.

AIME

You think it's a big joke, but I want that letter. You never know what they want. One minute be this, the next be that. They have me turning somersaults inside myself.
(To her)
When that man returns, I don't want you giving him any excuse to get angry. He must be frustrated but not angry, like today.

VIOLA

He wasn't angry.

AIME

He called you a black madonna.

VIOLA

He smiled and waved the letter and his eyes glittered.

AIME

He wasn't resentful, as if he just been forced into a large donation?

VIOLA

He bowed and blew me a kiss and shut the door firmly, but politely.

AIME

Turn off that music!
    (SHE turns it off)
Bring in the next!
    (SHE exits, returns with eight-year-old doll.)
Not that one! He's the one that went to the river! His lies about Fred and Bubber and Tyson being with those men!
    (SHE puts doll down, exits.)
Lies! You said they called out to you? Asked when I was coming to join them? I know they never said that because those men never utter a sound! Not even to you! You have nothing to say to that, do you. They were troublemakers. They embarrassed people with their anger, violated people with their questions. They caused whole rooms to go silent! If they ended up at the river, it's their own damn fault! But don't try to put me in their category. I get along just fine. I'm quite happy. Despite your provocations.
    (VIOLA has returned with the nine-year-old doll and stands watching AIME.)
What are you standing there for? Begin!

VIOLA

    (As child)
What if Taipei fell?

AIME

It won't fall, David. Joel.

VIOLA

If a plane fell, what if there were no survivors?

AIME

Albert!

VIOLA

If the honest man didn't take the flowers...?

AIME

Reginald!

VIOLA

And the postman...?

AIME

I won't have it! No more names! Silence!
        (Turns on TV)

VIOLA

Aime...

AIME

Silence! I'm on to all of you! Trying to provoke me! Cause trouble between me and them. Don and I are great friends. He is the closest friend I ever had. I won't have you question him, none of your insinuations! We are firm!
        (A silence. The TV glows gray as AIME and VIOLA are motionless.)
Silly to get worked up over a name. He was a boy, a child like any other. He had charm, that's all. He used it. People think little black boys are cute. They dote on them. Nothing special in that.
        (Sighs, turns up TV)

NEWSCASTER VOICE

In Formosa today fighting was sparse around Taipei. Our forces repulsed a thrust at the key salient of Cu'an Twa. Enemy losses were high. Closer to home, the unrest that has gripped the Phillipine capital of Manilla came to an end today. Civic elections were postponed and all political activity banned. In taking over the reins of government General Thomas Shire declared, "We are here to preserve democracy." On the human side of the news Mrs. Elsie Johnson has this incident to report.

INTERVIEWER

Mrs. Johnson, you were expecting a letter.

ELSIE

That is right, my husband's insurance check.

INTERVIEWER

And the postman came.

ELSIE

Yes, he did.

INTERVIEWER

And he refused to carry the letter up the stairs, so you said...

ELSIE

I said I can take it or leave it.

INTERVIEWER

And what was his response?

ELSIE

He said, "I am not walking up any flight of stairs for any white madonna." Then he bowed and left.

AIME

Madonna! Did you hear?

INTERVIEWER

And he did not return.

ELSIE

No, he did not. I waited seven hours at the head of the stairs, but he failed to return. Then this evening as I was lighting the candles for dinner, I tripped over a chair and I called out Mercy.

INTERVIEWER

And that is when the doorbell rang.

ELSIE

It was him. He brought my check up the stairs. I know it was my little plea for mercy that brought him back.

(AIME turns sound of TV down)

AIME

Go to the door.

VIOLA

What? Why?

AIME

Do as I say.

(SHE crosses to door)

Mercy.

(HE waits)

Mercy.

(No response)

It's not enough. Get the candles.

VIOLA

Are you crazy? It happened in some farm town far away.

AIME

He said the same words. I won't walk up any stairs for any white madonna.

VIOLA

I am no white madonna.

AIME

Will you stop picking on petty points?

(SHE exits, re-enters with candles)

Light them.

(THEY light the candles)

Say it.

VIOLA

Say what?

AIME

What she said.

VIOLA

Mercy.

AIME

With feeling.

VIOLA

Mercy.

AIME

No, no, as if you had just tripped over a chair.

VIOLA

Mercy!

(THEY wait)

AIME

(Puts chair before her)

Trip over this. Then say mercy, and he will come.

VIOLA

Oh, Aime, where is my child? They took him without mercy!

AIME

Viola, please...

VIOLA

He was my first! So hard getting him out of me! Aime!

VIOLA(CONT'D)
(SHE cries. HE takes her to record player, turns up music.)

MUSIC:"Dock Of The Bay",Otis Redding.

(SHE dances and weeps. HE puts chair in middle of room, trips over it, candle in hand.)

AIME

Mercy!

VIOLA

I was young! I didn't know about babies! He scared me when he got his fevers! I wanted to have fun, but he was there!

AIME

Mercy!

VIOLA

I made him strange! He knew he frightened me, so he went away! I made him go.

AIME

Mercy!

VIOLA

I'll be better with the next! I'll know what to do! But he suffered!

AIME

Mercy!

VIOLA

Help me, Aime, get me another child!

                    AIME
Mercy!

                    VIOLA
Help me!

                    AIME
            (Knocks over a chair with a doll)
Mercy!

                    VIOLA
            (Picks up doll)
Oh, my baby fell.

                    AIME
Mercy!

        (In this last section as the music plays and the
TV VOICES continue, AIME lurches about the room knocking
over dolls and chairs with VIOLA following behind, frantically
replacing them in position, in vain.)

                    AIME
Mercy!

                    VIOLA
Oh, baby!

                    AIME
Mercy!

                    VIOLA
Mercy!

                    AIME

Mercy!

                    VIOLA

Mercy! My baby!

                    AIME

Mercy!

        (The room is a chaos of chairs, dolls, and sounds)

                    CURTAIN

                    END OF ACT II

ACT III

LIGHTS:Up on The Studio. The next day.

(At rise AIME is sitting in his chair. DON paces back and forth.)

DON

It was a complete success. Boy she never knew what hit her. Of course, it wasn't exactly the way I planned it. There was this... Boy, was she surprised. What about you? Did you remember your boy's name?

AIME

Oh, yes, yes...

DON

What is it?

AIME

What is what?

DON

His name.

AIME

Bob. Robert.

DON

Then everything is settled

AIME

Everything is fine.

DON

Yes, with me, too.

AIME

Good.

DON

I really feel myself. I feel the power running through me.

AIME

I am at peace. I really am.

DON

Was that his secret?

AIME

Whose secret?

DON

Your boy's secret. You said he had a secret.

AIME

Oh, that. Well... His secret.

DON

You're lying to me. You didn't remember his name.

AIME

Well, I....

DON

You are never honest with me, are you?

AIME

The postman came. With the letter.
            (Points to prop closet)
He called my wife a black madonna and left.

DON

He didn't deliver?

AIME

Elsie Johnson tripped and cried mercy and he returned. We cried mercy till dawn, then collapsed on the floor.

DON

He never returned?
                (AIME shakes his head)
Impossible.
                (AIME shrugs. DON crosses to prop closet, takes
out letter)
This letter?

AIME

"Genoa is a big joke."

DON

The same. Your wife did something wrong. She said a wrong word or made a wrong gesture... He delivered to my wife. This is a very serious charge you are making. I only hope you can back it up with proof. Otherwise you are in serious trouble.
                (A silence moment)
Well, say something. You people are always silent when something needs to be said.

AIME

She played the scene wrong.

DON

Of course she did.
                (A pause)
You are lying! Never anything but lies from your black mouth!

                              AIME

Please, don't.
                    (HE rises)
Don't say things like that.

          (DON rushes to closet, takes out rifle and works
mechanism repeatedly till AIME retreats into his chair)

                              DON

Are you afraid?

                              AIME

Yes.

                              DON

No, you are not.

                              AIME

No I am not.

                              DON

Oh, that mocking voice!
                    (Works rifle)
Here's one I invented last night. A wicker basket with a round
opening in the bottom. Two ropes lead up from the basket
to a pulley on the ceiling. She sits, fully clothed but without
underpants in the basket. I lie down on the floor and raise her up
to the ceiling. I center myself beneath, then... My gosh, the look of
surprise in her eyes. I surprise her! I see nothing! Her stocking,
I see her stockings! A bit of white leg, too. But the rest hidden,
dark, obscure! Beautiful, no?

          (AIME nods)

                         DON (Continued)

Say it.

                          AIME
Beautiful.

                          DON
What is?

                          AIME
Your invention.

                          DON
And the risk? I stake everything. The slightest inaccuracy, the
variation of a fraction, a minute change in wind speed and I am
crippled for life, seedless, empty! Say the risk is beautiful. No,
better exquisite.

                          AIME
The risk is exquisite.

                          DON
More emotion.

                          AIME
What an exquisite risk.

                          DON
Once more. Use my personal pronoun.

                          AIME
You! What an exquisite risk!

                          DON
One sentence!

                          AIME
One sentence!

DON

Up to your trickery again!?
(AIME looks blank)
What an exquisite risk you devised.

AIME

What an exquisite risk you devised.

DON

When you get the correct grammar you lose all emotion.

AIME

What an exquisite risk you devised!

DON

You are all huddled up! Open up! Show me with your body!

AIME

(Shouts, twisting his body distortedly)
What an exquisite risk you devised!

DON

No truth! None! You never give me what I want!
(Returns rifle to the closet,suddenly apologetic)
I will requisition another version for you.
(Crosses to AIME)
Wouldn't you like that?

AIME

Sit down. Try not to be afraid for a moment. Let us talk as men together.

DON

As friends.

AIME

We're not friends.

DON

I can only speak for myself, but I consider myself your friend.

AIME

We might have been. We might yet be, but from the first day when you corrected my speech and I let you, we've been something else to each other.
(DON looks anxiously at control booth)
Sit down. I'll whisper.
(DON sits)
I need your help.

DON

I can't open the letter for you. It's not allowed.

AIME

Listen to me. Remember my name is Aime which is love, so you know I mean no harm.

DON

If you mean no harm, why do you always taunt me?

AIME

I 'll get to that. For now, though, try to be at ease. Be with me just for one sentence at a time.
(A moment as HE gathers his thoughts)
My mind is a madhouse of names and questions. I try to take food, but they vomit it out. I sit to rest, but they drive me from the chair. I want to be with you, but they dance between us, confusing my eyes and my mind even more.

DON

We have the answers.

AIME

I believe it. I want to believe it. But how can I know for certain until I reach down and shake his secret soul till it shatters in a thousand fraudulent pieces?

DON

You know what they did to the colored fellow in Studio 19. Do you want that to happen?

AIME

This morning as my wife and I lay exhausted on the floor, she begged me for another child. She reached out and pleaded to be taken. The first stream of daylight gleamed on her legs. All the sights and sounds of love came into me. It's most beautiful in the morning with one you love. You join together in the beginning of time ...

DON

Stop it. I won't listen.

AIME

... But I couldn't do it! I turned away! My mind was here, locked in this room! My eyes saw nothing but what lies on the shelf in there. Ask them. Ask them, if you may open it. They listen to you. They respect you. Do it and I will never taunt you again. Never smile to terrify you. Never feign ignorance to frustrate you. Never sulk to punish you or ask innocent questions that destroy you.

Those are my last defenses. I 'll give them up. I 'll praise you exultantly. I 'll cower joyfully under your threats. I will imitate you with an eagerness that will astound you. I will be yours. Completely. Eternally.
            (Gestures DON to go forward. DON rises and goes
              to center of floor, looks out to the control booth)
Ask them.
            (Don hesitates)
May I open the letter and read it to Aime.

DON

What if asking is not allowed? Then that.
                    (Nods toward blue light)
                    AIME

It won't.

                    DON

How do you know? You don't know.
                    (HE begins shivering)
I didn't surprise her last night. I tried, but...

                    AIME

I know.

                    DON

You knew I was lying? You didn't punish me with it?

                    AIME

My first act of friendship.

                    DON

I can trust your promises? If you do as you say, then I won't have
to try to surprise her. I can do it here.

                    AIME

With me.

                    DON

You won't object? Will you wear a skirt and stockings...?

                    AIME

And high heels.

                    DON

But no...

AIME

Nothing underneath. Go on.

DON

But it's immoral. Doesn't that bother you?

AIME

I 've gone too far to turn back.

DON

(Wheels around)

Why do you say that? She said that last night. Did she tell you to
say it?

AIME

Say what?

DON

Ooh, just in time! You almost had me! I almost asked them!
(Laughs)

That would have finished me! Very clever! You are infernally
shrewd, but I caught you! You gave yourself away!

AIME

What are you talking about?

DON

Yes, yes, always pretend innocence when your plot is being
unmasked. That way I'll never know for sure. But I do know. You
and she arranged this whole scheme to get me out of the way.
(Laughs again)

Oh, those heartfelt phrases, that passionate story! All concocted
to trap me! Yes, I ask them, then the blue light, I disappear, and
it is all yours. Yours and hers. Brilliant. But not brilliant enough.
You're dealing here with a man who is a bit of a plotter himself. I
caught you!

AIME

No, Don, it's your fear talking! Don't listen to it!

DON

My fear has protected me! It warns me! You almost robbed me of
it!
        (Laughs)
But I caught you with your hand in my soul. Didn't I? Didn't I?
        (Walks around the room laughing)
Ha-ha! Just try to get that letter! Just you try!
        (Laughs again)
Planted" poisonous questions" in your mind! Marvelous! I almost
wanted to save you!
        (Laughs)
I 'm not angry. I should be, but I'm not. I'm enjoying it! Let's have
more! Add a little
spice to the proceedings!

YELLOW SIGNAL.

LIGHT:Flashes.

DON

Duty calls
        (Crosses to schedule chart)
The Sole Survivor. Come on, you consummate schemer and help
your victim prepare.
        (They cross to prop closet)
Ah, wait. I'll hand them to you.
        (Takes out jackets, magazines, hands one of each to
AIME, closes the closet)
I won't close it. That would snuff out the" poisonous questions".

AIME

What if this once you didn't survive?

DON

Ah, toxic question number one. Answer: I always survive. I have
secret powers. If I don't survive it puts them in question. Set up
the chairs.

(AIME places the two chairs in the center of the
circle, facing out to the control booth)

AIME

Oh, God, it's happening. Stop it. Take it. Be silent, black man.

DON
(Sitting in chair, jacket on, magazine in lap)
Don't be silent, black man. Speak!

AIME

What if there were two survivors?

DON

Very good. Confuse everyone, cast doubt on the entire concept
that each individual can be the SOLE SURVIVOR.. Give it to
everyone, then it's worth nothing. Throw us back into primordial
panic. Fear of the sky, of the green oceans, of the very earth we
walk. Good. But I wouldn't suggest it too loudly. They might not
consider it as funny as I do.

(AIME sits)

AIME

What if I saw the wing shuddering and warned the pilot?

DON

The charade has gone far enough. You do not see it coming. It
has to be a sudden jolt, a rip, the whining dive earthward. We are
reading.
(HE reads his magazine)

                              AIME

Donald... Dorian...?

                              DON

No talking.

                              AIME

Has it started?

                              DON

I will report you.

                              AIME

I told you this would happen!

                              DON

Silence! I'm not falling for any more of your pretenses. Prepare
your part. A blue sky, yellow sun above and white clouds below.
We are reading.

            (THEY read in silence.)

            LIGHTS: The RED LIGHT flashes.

            SOUND: The steady steady WHISTLE OF AIR
            for a long beat, then CARRUMP.

                              AIME

What was that?

                              DON

I don't know. Look, the wing!

            SOUND:The Jets wind up into a SCREAM.

            (THEY plunge downward.)

            LIGHTS:Green and red lights whirl around
            the circle.

                         DON
God! Help! God!

                         AIME
God.

                         DON
No! Nooooo!

                      BLACKOUT.

        SOUND:Silence. No sound of crash.

           LIGHTS:Up on circle.

            (DON lies on the floor, his chair tipped over next to
him. AIME lies crumpled beneath his chair)

DON
We crashed.
            (HE looks around)
I am alive… I made it… I am alive!
            (Gets to his feet, winces)
Ow! My arm is broken.
            (Surveys the wreckage, then AIME)
All gone. Gee, he was with me just a moment ago. Sitting next
to me reading the financial section. Gee, I guess he did not have
secret powers.

      SOUND: sirens, trucks, helicopters.

DON
Here come the rescuers. Won't they be surprised to find me alive.

      SOUND: MEN'S VOICES amid the wreckage.

                              DON

Here! Here I am! I'm alive!

                              AIME

                    (Stirs, faintly)

I'm... I'm alive... alive...

                  CONTROLLER'S VOICE

What is that?

                              AIME

                    (Rises to his feet)

I'm alive!

                  CONTROLLER'S VOICE

Cut! Station signal! Cut!

                              AIME

I'm alive, too!

(DON rushes over, clamps a hand over AIME's mouth. THEY stay
frozen for a moment.)

            SOUND: Overly loud cocktail music comes from the
right speaker.

                  (DON lets go.)

                              DON

It was no pretense. You were serious. Well, you're in for it now.

                              AIME

The blue light?

                              DON

As ye sow, so shall ye reap.

AIME

I didn't mean it. I tried to keep still. A blue light?

DON

They never play that music unless there's trouble. This was no slip either.

AIME

I'm sorry! It burst out of me!

DON

You certainly have gone too far. But not to the end. They will take you there.

AIME

Where?

DON

Wherever.

AIME

It hasn't flashed yet. Is that a good sign?

DON

They have to check the tapes first. It takes a few minutes.

LIGHTS:Come up on room.

AIME

They don't do that when there's a blue. They keep only the circle lit.

DON
(Crosses to chart)
Might be a change in procedure.

AIME

What does it say? No change in procedure.

CONTROLLER'S VOICE

The tapes show no video of him doing it. We were tight on you,
Don. Only a very faint audio, very faint, "I'm alive" which will not
be noticed.

DON

(To control booth)

Excuse me. I'm not questioning your judgment, but this was no
accident.

CONTROLLER'S VOICE

Aime, would you drop in to room 104 when you have a moment?

AIME

Are they still going to handle my boy's arrangements? What I did
won't affect that, will it?

DON

Did you hear me? He planned it.

AIME

(To Control Booth)

I didn't! It was a mistake! Do you hear me?

(Silence)

DON

He's gone.

AIME

Room 104, who's there?

DON

Nobody.

AIME

What happens there? A black chair?

DON

Nothing happens. You go in, stand wait, and leave.

AIME

Why do they want me to go there?

DON

So you know that something will happen.

AIME

When? Where?

DON

I don't know.

AIME

Another room? With a slab and trough? They don't tell you anything?

       (HE crosses toward DON who backs off toward the closet)

DON

You simply wait.

AIME

Wait for what?

SOUND:An offstage door opens and slams.

AIME
What was that?
       (To DON, who is backed up against the prop closet)
You're trying to terrify me again!

DON
       (Terrified)
Get back! Don't come near me!

AIME
       (Backing off)
I won't! I won't! But please, don't get me angry!

DON
More of your trickeries!

AIME
       (Retreating to chair)
I'll be good. No more questions! I swear!

DON
       (Remembers)
Oh, my gosh!
       (Crosses to schedule chart)
I was afraid of that!
       (Back to prop closet, addresses Control Booth)
He lost his boy! An automobile... There's an auto in the scene...!

TAIPEI OFFICER
Withdraw... Withdraw... Cover fire, sector C, give us cover...

DON
He's frightened! He admitted it! He did!

AIME
Withdrawing? From Taipei?

                              DON
Do you hear? He doesn't believe we'll hold Taipei! He said it! We
have the airpower, the sea… The sea power…The…

                     STEWARDESS' VOICE
Ladies and gentleman, below is the majestic Grand Canyon.
                (A loud CARRUMPP)
What's that? The wing?
                (Scream of diving jets)
My god!

PASSENGERS' VOICES
Help! The wing! Bobby!

DON AIME
Nooooooo! Nooooooo!

SOUND:The WHINE and SCREAMS grow deafening, then silence.

                              DON
                (Grabs gun from closet, works mechanism
feverishly, paces up and down before AIME)
I thought it up this morning! A circular booth with five round
openings. Each one leads to a cubicle … …. .
                (His tone grows staccato)
I stand in the booth, ready. The cubicles contain one woman, her
and four maddened cobras! All ready! She, without panties, the
cobras hooded, the walls turn, like the cylinders of a pistol…!

                             AIME
                (To control booth, as HE cowers in his chair)
Survivors? Any?

                              DON
I must choose, luck pure luck brilliant luck, courage, greatness,
or…!

                              AIME

Survivors?

                              DON

If I lose, the angry teeth in my flesh, headache, nausea, limbs
jerking...!

                          CONTROLLER
                (Reads)
Change title 324 to read "The Defense of Manilla."

                              DON

Paralysis choked breath darkness...!

                              AIME

Taipei has fallen!?

                              DON

The risk great, say it, say it, say it before I blow your stinking
brains out!

                              AIME

The risk...

                              DON

No! Tricks! More tricks!
                    (AIME heads for the prop closet. DON blocks his
way)
Back! Back!

                    LIGHTS:YELLOW LIGHT flashes.

Wait! You can't let him! He's too frightened! He wants the letter!
He's going to open the letter! He's going to open the letter!

(As HE trains gun on AIME, HE frantically takes from the closet the props for the next scene, a wooden cross and a bouquet of flowers, throwing them to the floor. AIME picks them up)

AIME

What is happening? Taipei?

DON

Look in his eyes? You will see!

AIME
(Calls out to booth)
No survivors? The boy was right?

DON

Don't you hear him? Aren't you listening?

LIGHTS:RED SIGNAL flashes.

DON

Wait!

(HE drops the gun. BOTH MEN pick up their props and rush into the circle.
THEY play the scene at machine-gun tempo, jerkily, moving spastically in terrorized steps at and around EACH OTHER.)

AIME

My father was killed by a car...

DON

Didn't he look both ways...

AIME

He didn't look up. Survivors...

                    DON
Up how can a car hit you from up...?

                    AIME
It fell on him in the garage in Taipei where the boy...

                    DON
... You must have grieved terribly...

                    AIME
... The letter...

                    DON
... Grieved terribly...

            CONTROLLER'S VOICE
Dialogue check on Studio 4.

                    DON
...My father died, I cried for two days back, back...

                    AIME
... His name on the spit on his grave...

                    DON
... Very clever but you must understand...

                    AIME
... His name!
            (HE breaks for the closet. DON beats him to it,
reaches for the pistol. THEY grapple for it)

            CONTROLLER'S VOICE
Cut! Cut! Mountain Scene! Cut!

SOUND:A shot rings out.

(DON falls dead.)

SOUND:Cocktail music plays loudly.

LIGHTS:A whirling blue light whips around
the studio.

SOUND: A siren wails.

(AIME runs to the door. It is locked. HE runs back.
Black forms writhe on the walls.)

LIGHTS: Green lights blink on and off.

AIME
No, no, please!
(The din increases)
No!
(It grows to a nightmare of lights and sounds.
AIME runs chaotically back and forth. The nightmare increases to
a maddening deafness)
Nooooo!
(HE shoots out the blue light, which starts-)

LIGHTS: the red and yellow lights whirling.

(HE shoots them out.)

CONTROLLER'S VOICE
Emergency! Emergency!

(AIME shoots out the LOUDSPEAKER. Suddenly
there is SILENCE.

LIGHTS:Up on room.

(AIME stands there, violent, ready. Stillness SILENCE. In Negro dialect.)

AIME

Come on! I'm ready! Well, come on!
(Silence)
What you waiting for? You gonna scare me some more before you kill me? You can't scare me no more!
(HE waits. Nothing happens)
What's the matter, baby, you 'fraid to come in and get me? Yeah, I got a gun now! Sure do make things different, don't it?
(Silence)
Hey, you there? Say something!
(Silence)
You wouldn't be playing possum on old Aime, would you?
(HE crosses to the door. It opens to his touch. HE calls out...)
Hey, anybody here?
(HE peers out into the hallway)
Hallway's empty. Maybe I scared 'em off.
(Calls out)
You' layin' for me out there, huh?
(No response)
Cain't stay in here forever. Coming at you, baby!
(HE dashes out. The stage is empty and silent for a few moments, then offstage)
Hey! Where is everybody? Hey, anybody home?
(HE laughs)
I must have scared them 'em off.
(On mike)
Hello? Hello? This is Studio 4. Studio 1, you there?
(To himself)
What's that cat's name in 1? Trimbell. Hey, Trimbell, you there?
(Silence)
Studio 2? You there, 2?

(Silence)

5, Studio 5, answer me... 12... 16... 34...?

(Silence)

Hey, you white motherfuckers,, you there?

(HE laughs)

You there, you red-neck bastards?

(Laughs again)

You li'l ole whitefuck?

(Laughs)

Ain't no white shit 'round here!

(Laughs raucously, re-enters)

I am gonna open up that never-open-that letter.

(Crosses to prop closet, takes out letter)

His name. Oh, yeah, his name shall reveal the universe! The sun and the stars are mine! And the heavens shall be too and the corners shall be made light!

AIME(CONT'D)

(HE opens the letter, reads...)

That's all? ...

(Reads aloud)

"Welcome to Genoa."

(Grabs microphone)

This all? All there is? No! Got to be here! I killed a man! Can't leave like this! ... A clue, an initial! ... First initial! ... I'll dig the rest! ... I'll know! It won't matter I'm alone! ... Something.

(Falls back amid the debris)

Nothing!

(Looks to see props)

All make believe! Ha-ha-ha! I brought it down with my own hands! Ha-ha-ha!

(Crosses to DON's body)

Come on buddy, you ain't dead! All make believe! Come on, get up!

(The body does not move)

The bullets were real. So was he. Just him and me. We made it all, and I killed him. I am... The Sole Survivor...

(HE chuckles)

Me! The Sole...

(It broadens to a laugh)

.... Survivor!

(stops still,hears the silence)

Oh, baby, I'm alone. Alone...

(Looks around,then)

After the fields, after the factory, after Washington Avenue, after the studio, after it's all mine, the power and the victories and my face in the mirror of the world... After journeying thru it all where have I arrived? Eh, Sojourner, where have you arrived? After all the truths, what is the final one, the one that makes a joke of all the rest?! ...

(He smiles,knowing)

And you, Sojourner, have arrived!

(HE is silent)

Albert? ... Adrian?

(HE rises, paces up and down)

Arthur? ... Allen? ... Andre? ... Alex? ...

FINAL CURTAIN